OVER
FLOW

Clint Sprague

with Ardythe Kolb

OVERFLOW
living a Spirit-empowered life
© 2016, 2018 by Clint Sprague and Ardythe Kolb

Cover design by Jonathan Rodriguez and Kristen Brinks

"We all need to live with the abundance of the Holy Spirit that has been given to us as a gift from God. Pastor Clint lives this life and I'm so grateful he wrote this book. May the Holy Spirit burst forth from its pages and saturate every part of our lives."

Brady Boyd,
Senior Pastor of New Life Church in Colorado Springs
Author of *Addicted to Busy* and *Sons & Daughters*

"*Overflow* is a book whose time has come. God said in Joel 2, that He would 'pour out His Spirit on all flesh'. This book helps us flow with what God is doing in our day....the last days. It will bless, encourage and help equip you to be all God has called you to be. I highly recommend this book."

Pastor Duane VanderKlok
Resurrection Life Church
Author of *Unleashing the Force of Favor*
and *Get the Junk Out of Your Trunk*

"God desires to personally lead, comfort, teach and empower you through the Holy Spirit! In *Overflow*, Pastor Clint takes us on a Biblical journey into knowing and walking with the Holy Spirit. His energy, stories, and practical application will inspire you to *Overflow*! This is a must-read for every follower of Jesus!"

David Perkins
USA Director at Every Home for Christ
and Founder of Desperation Conferences
@DavidPerkins27

"My friend Clint Sprague has written one of the most simple, practical, and biblically based introductions to the Holy Spirit's nature and ministry I have ever read. *Overflow* informs without weirdness, and stirs a hunger for the Holy Spirit by showing access to everybody. Clint is a proven voice to this generation with more than two decades of faithfulness in missions, evangelism, youth ministry, and church leadership. This book is simply an overflow of his lifestyle. I am very excited about the release of his first book."

Dean Sherman
Dean of the College of Christian Ministries for the
University of the Nations
Author of *Relationships* and *Spiritual Warfare*

"*Overflow* is an encouraging and empowering book that will challenge you to delve deeper into a relationship with the Holy Spirit. Written by a pastor with an evangelist's heart, this book is an attainable read with a challenging message all at the same time. I highly recommend it."

Lee Cummings
Lead Pastor of Radiant Church
President of RLCI Association Of Churches
Author of *Be Radiant*

Contents

1

Impact of Overflow

Say, "Overflow."

Go ahead, say, "OVERFLOW" out loud, right now! You can do this!

Does that feel strange? I remind people at Life-Mission Church that Christianity is not a spectator sport. I expect them to participate and connect with me. I feel the same way about this book, so go ahead and say, "Overflow!"

The word *overflow* means to spill out over the limits or edges of a container because the container is too full. What does *overflow* make you think of? It's easy to picture all sorts of things that can overflow—coffee mugs, bathtubs, even lakes and rivers.

But the overflow we will focus on comes from the Bible. The Apostle Paul wrote about this sort of overflow in the book of Romans:

> I pray that God, the source of hope, will fill you completely with joy and peace because you trust in Him. Then you will overflow with confident hope through the power of the Holy Spirit (Romans 15:13 NLT).

Think about that. We can be completely filled with joy and peace—so full we overflow with confident hope, because we trust in God. Does that sound good to you? It does to me! Why *wouldn't* we want to overflow with hope that comes from the power of the Holy Spirit?

Paul knew God's heart and realized that He wants so much more than for us to just barely scrape by. "Well, I made it through another day. Guess that's the best I can expect in this fallen world." No! God's passion is for all of us to be full of joy and peace through the indwelling Holy Spirit. When that takes place, we overflow with confident hope.

So, what happens when a person overflows with joy and peace and hope? Let me tell you how that kind of overflow in one man's life affected me.

When I was seventeen years old I worked for my dad in Idaho. At that time I'd been kicked out of one school and was about to flunk at another. I was into drugs, had violent tendencies, and tried whatever looked good to me at the moment—all kinds of stupid things.

My dad did some business with a cowboy named Lin, who owned a body shop. Lin wore scuffed boots, a wide-brimmed western hat, and had a belt buckle big enough to eat breakfast on. But what I really noticed was that his life was full of joy and peace and hope. At first I thought he was weird. *No one's that happy! This dude must be on something.*

As I got to know Lin, I realized that what made him different was an intense faith. His beliefs went deep and affected everything he did. When Lin said he'd pray for somebody, he really prayed. And everyone knew they could count on him for help if they had problems, like a truck stuck in a ditch or a worn-out tractor that needed an overhaul.

Lin wasn't perfect and he didn't pretend to be. But somewhere along the way he became convinced that Jesus is who He says He is and does what He says He'll do. And Lin fell completely in love with the Lord.

When Lin met me, he didn't stumble over my obvious problems, even though I was a longhaired, crazy kid with a rebellious mindset. Some people might have lectured me, "You need to clean up and get your act together!" But my clothes and attitude must not have been major issues to Lin. He never tried to preach at me. He just talked to me about God like they were good friends.

One of his favorite expressions first thing every day was, "Praise the Lord! It's good to be alive in the Great Northwest!" Sometimes he quoted a Bible verse he'd read that morning or told me what the Lord was doing in his life.

Lin seemed to value me. He even believed in me. I never felt that before from anyone except my mom.

Lin encouraged me and spoke hope into my life. "Clint, God has a purpose for you. You're not alone. You don't have to keep on doing the things you've been doing." He saw possibilities for me that I sure couldn't see.

Everyone who spent time with Lin was impacted by the power of the Holy Spirit that overflowed and spilled out of him. That overflow splashed onto people like me—I'm here today because of the overflow from Lin's life. And one of the exciting things for me to think about is that if I've influenced anyone, it's a direct result of a cowboy in Idaho who simply loved God and wanted others to know Him. Lin was a living example of Romans 15:13.

Can We Overflow?

Paul's prayer for the Roman Christians is as true for us today as it was when he wrote it. I want you to keep this verse in mind while you read the rest of this book. Look at it again.

> I pray that God, the source of hope, will fill you completely with joy and peace because you trust in Him. Then you will overflow with confident hope through the power of the Holy Spirit.

Think about some of the words—words like *joy* and *peace* and *confident hope*.

The word *peace* implies a calm harmony that leads to *joy*—something much deeper than just feeling happy. When we're filled with peace there's no room for worry or anxiety. *Confident hope* involves anticipation, expectation, and assurance.

What does it look like to overflow? How does it affect others when we're *too* full of the confident hope that comes from being filled with the Holy Spirit? Is it actually possible for us to be so full of God that we overflow with the Holy Spirit in every area of life?

Scripture clearly teaches that each day is an opportunity to be refilled with God's Holy Spirit. In everything we do and say, we can be filled to the point that we spill out onto the world around us. What if our attitudes and motives and decisions were always full of Him—full to the point of overflow?

Sometimes we are too full of ourselves. When that happens, there's no room for the Holy Spirit to empower us. If He's crowded out, we come up short of the overflow God wants.

In some versions of the Bible, the word *overflow* is translated *abound*. I like that. It means to have enough with more to spare, to flourish, or thrive, to have no lack. If we don't flourish, we'll dry up and wither. Would you rather overflow or wilt like a plant that needs water?

Paul wrote his letters to the new believers of the first century, but everything God offered them is still available for us. I encourage you to open your heart to hear what the Holy Spirit wants to say to you as you read this book. Erase any predetermined notions and concentrate on the Lord, who always has our best interests in mind. Listen for His whisper in your heart, and let the clear message of Scripture guide you.

Say, "Overflow!"

2

Meet John "The Baptist"

As we focus on overflowing with the power of the Holy Spirit, let's go to the beginning of the New Testament and look at John the Baptist.

Before John was conceived, the angel Gabriel appeared to Zechariah, John's father, with the news that he and his wife would have a child:

> The angel said to him, "Do not be afraid, Zacharias, for your prayer is heard; and your wife Elizabeth will bear you a son, and you shall call his name John. And you will have joy

and gladness, and many will rejoice at his birth. For he will be great in the sight of the Lord. . . He will also be filled with the Holy Spirit even from his mother's womb" (Luke 1:13-15).

Zechariah and Elizabeth were old—too old to start a family—but age doesn't matter to God. Several stories in the Bible show how He surprised senior citizens with miraculous babies, and in each case the child became a special gift to the world.

The Genesis family album shows Abraham and Sarah with their son, Isaac, born when Abraham was 100 years old, and Sarah was 90 (Genesis 17:17, 21:5).

Isaac's son, Jacob, married Rachael, who grew old and felt like a failure, unable to bear a son. Then she gave birth to Joseph, who eventually saved the Hebrew people from starvation. His story begins in Genesis 30.

The Prophet Samuel's parents, Elkanah and Hannah, almost gave up hope of ever having a child, but God changed their perspective and presented them with a son in their old age (1 Samuel 1).

Then, in the New Testament, John entered the world. His mother Elizabeth was related to Mary, who would become the mother of Jesus. When Mary visited Elizabeth while both women were pregnant, we're told that John leaped in Elizabeth's womb and she was filled with the Holy Spirit (Luke 1:41).

Imagine how awesome that experience must have been for these women! Mary knew a miracle was happening in her life and Gabriel told her Elizabeth was also going to have a baby. As soon as Mary arrived at Elizabeth's home, they both realized this was a divine moment. In Luke 1:43, Elizabeth wondered, out loud, "But why is this granted to me, that the mother of my Lord should come to me?" Think about that. Before they had time to chat, Elizabeth knew, by the power of the Holy Spirit, that Mary was carrying the Son of God—the long-awaited Messiah.

We don't know anything about John's childhood or youth, but when he became an adult he was zealous to fulfill God's purpose for his life. From what the Bible tells us about John, it's hard to imagine a more unconventional character to pave the way for the Messiah. He was definitely not your typical seeker-friendly pastor. What a first impression this dude must have made!

John was about thirty years old when he began to preach, and he was a wild man—about as counter-culture as you can get. He wandered throughout the wilderness dressed in camel's hair, wearing a leather belt around his waist, eating locusts and wild honey. Both Matthew and Mark mention these odd facts, so there must be some significance. The custom at that time was for mourners to wear robes made from coarse hair. We know John mourned over the sin he saw in people. Maybe his clothes and diet revealed a lack of interest in anything except his need to obey the Holy Spirit and fulfill his purpose to prepare the way for the Lord.

Based on his appearance, if John lived in your neighborhood you might warn your kids to avoid him. He wasn't a distinguished gentleman who commanded respect merely by his looks. He wasn't a polished speaker, and he certainly didn't worry about keeping his words politically correct. John called the

Pharisees and Sadducees, the religious leaders of the day, a "brood of vipers" (Matthew 3:7). And he infuriated King Herod with a blunt accusation about Herod's immoral relationship with his sister-in-law (Mark 6:17-18).

So why do you suppose people streamed out from the towns and villages to hear John? It had to be the power of the Holy Spirit that overflowed from him.

One time when Jesus talked about John, He said:

> "What did you go into the wilderness to see? A reed shaken by the wind? But what did you go out to see? A man clothed in soft garments? Indeed, those who wear soft clothing are in kings' houses. But what did you go out to see? A prophet? Yes, I say to you, and more than a prophet" (Matthew 11:7-9).

Jesus Himself referred to John as "The Baptist" (Matthew 11:11) and declared that he was the fulfillment of a prophecy recorded by Malachi over 400 years earlier:

> "Behold I send My messenger, and he will prepare the way before Me" (Malachi 3:1).

John's message was simple, but it aroused multitudes. He proclaimed in a loud voice, "Repent, for the kingdom of heaven is at hand" (Matthew 3:2).

People from all over the region, commoners and high-class citizens alike, headed to the desert area near the Jordan River to hear what he had to say. Many of them repented and were baptized.

John Preached the Baptism in the Holy Spirit.

In Mark 1:7-8, John the Baptist told the crowds:

> "Someone is coming soon who is greater than I am—so much greater that I'm not even worthy to stoop down like a slave and untie the straps of his sandals. I baptize you with water, but he will baptize you with the Holy Spirit" (NLT).

We know from the rest of Scripture that he was talking about Jesus.

Of all the things John could have said about Jesus, he zeroed in on the fact that Jesus would baptize them with the Holy Spirit. Isn't that interesting! It's clear that this was a big deal to God.

The word *baptize* comes from the Greek *baptizo*. It means to dip so as to change, to immerse, submerge, or completely fill. John was saying that Jesus Christ would totally immerse them in the Holy Spirit, the same way John immersed them in water.

John's baptism—plunging people into the Jordan River—was a public declaration of their repentance. When we baptize people at LifeMission Church, we do the same thing. Believers step into the baptismal and a pastor dunks them into the water, and then raises them up again. It's an outward expression of what has already taken place in their hearts; a proclamation that they identify with Jesus' death, burial, and resurrection.

Water baptism helps us visualize what it means to be totally saturated with the Holy Spirit in order to overflow with joy and peace and confident hope through His power.

Say, "Overflow!"

3

The Holy Spirit and Jesus

If anyone understands the overflow of the Holy Spirit, it's Jesus. He's the One to look at when we want to learn how the Holy Spirit works. From Jesus' birth announcement to the day He was crucified, the Holy Spirit was a fundamental part of His life. The two were inseparable—the original dynamic duo.

The story of Jesus' earthly life started when the angel Gabriel visited Mary, a young girl who lived in Nazareth. His incredible message was that God had chosen her to be the mother of the Messiah. Mary's response was amazing. She didn't hesitate, except to ask, "But how can this happen? I am a virgin" (Luke 1:34 NLT).

> The angel replied, "The Holy Spirit will come upon you, and the power of the Most High will overshadow you. So the baby to be born will be holy, and he will be called the Son of God" (Luke 1:35 NLT).

The overflow of the Holy Spirit came from heaven to fill Mary with God Himself. Awesome!

Jesus was born in Bethlehem, where Joseph and Mary had to go for a census. We only know about a few incidents that happened when Jesus was a baby. The Bible tells of the shepherds' visit, the wise men who came from the East, and Jesus' dedication at the temple. An angel warned Joseph in a dream to escape to Egypt because of Herod's threats, and told him when it was safe to return to Israel. But other than these few incidents, Jesus' earliest years are a mystery.

His family must have seemed ordinary to people in their community. Mary and Joseph knew the miracle surrounding the birth of Jesus, but their neighbors may not have realized He was different from other children.

It would be fun to glimpse what Jesus was like as a child. Did He play with kids that lived nearby like other little boys? I think He liked to hang out in the workshop with Joseph, where He learned carpentry skills.

The only thing Scripture reveals about His youth is a frightening experience for Mary and Joseph when Jesus was twelve years old. Luke 2:41-51 tells the story. Their family went to Jerusalem every year for

Passover and that particular year, when they headed home, Jesus stayed behind. His parents didn't miss Him at first; they thought He was with some friends or relatives. But He didn't show up for meals, and when they asked the other travelers, no one had seen Him. So Mary and Joseph hurried back to the city and looked everywhere they could imagine. They hunted for three days, surely beside themselves with worry. If I were Joseph, I might have been thinking, *Great! God trusted me to raise His Son, and now I've lost Him!*

When Joseph and Mary finally found Jesus in the temple, talking to the teachers, we hear the worry in His mother's words. Mary said, "Young man, why have you done this to us? Your father and I have been half out of our minds looking for you" (Luke 2:48 MSG).

His reply, recorded in verse 49, must have confused His parents as much as His absence. He said, "Why were you looking for me? Didn't you know that I had to be here, dealing with the things of my Father?"

Jesus wasn't being cocky. He merely stated a fact. As far as we know His folks didn't punish Him—picture grounding the Son of God. Luke 2:51 tells us they returned to Nazareth and Jesus was obedient to them. Such respect by One who was probably wiser than His earthly parents is a sure sign of the Spirit of God. Even as a pre-teen, the Holy Spirit overflowed from Him to others.

The Holy Spirit at the Jordan River

Now fast-forward to Jesus' baptism when He was about thirty years old. He came to John the Baptist at the Jordan River and said, "John, baptize Me."

John must have felt totally overwhelmed, and tried to talk Him out of it. Imagine John saying, "Me? Baptize the Son of God? No way! I'm just supposed to get people ready for what You're going to do. I need to be baptized by You!"

But Jesus set him at ease. Can you see Jesus putting His arm around John's shoulders, searching his eyes? "It's okay, John. This is what the Father planned, to fulfill all righteousness" (Matthew 3:15). With that assurance, John agreed to baptize his Messiah. What an experience!

In the next verses we hear more about this event:

> When He had been baptized, Jesus came up immediately from the water; and behold, the heavens were opened to Him, and He saw the Spirit of God descending like a dove and alighting upon Him. And suddenly a voice came from heaven, saying, "This is My beloved Son, in whom I am well pleased" (Matthew 3:16-17).

Later, when people questioned John the Baptist, he said:

> "I saw the Spirit descending from heaven like a dove, and He remained upon Him. I did not know Him, but He who sent me to baptize with water said to me, 'Upon whom you see the Spirit descending and remaining on Him, this is He who baptizes with the Holy Spirit'" (John 1:32-33).

Think about the end of that verse. The clear implication is that Jesus will baptize others—that includes you and me—with the very same Holy Spirit that filled Him. I love that! And it shows how important being filled with the Holy Spirit is to God the Father.

John quoted what God told him. He didn't finish that statement with, "this is He who heals," or, "this is He who casts out demons," or, "this is He who brings the dead back to life." Obviously the Father wanted us to know that the baptism with the Holy Spirit is a major part of a normal Christian life.

Jesus Confounded the Tempter

Right after His water baptism, "Jesus was led by the Spirit into the wilderness to be tempted by the devil" (Matthew 4:1).

Let's be real. Even though I want to be led by the same Holy Spirit, I'm not crazy about the idea that He might take me to a desert for a meeting with Satan. That's not a thrilling prospect, but we all face temptation, and we can learn a lot about how to handle it by studying Jesus' amazing wisdom and strength during His forty-day wilderness experience.

Jesus didn't just confront a few minor-league demons in that desolate region. Satan himself used every temptation he could come up with—things he thought would be irresistible.

It's kind of ironic, but the Bible reminds us Jesus was hungry after fasting forty days. He'd been alone, with no food all that time, and the devil probably assumed Jesus was vulnerable; it was a perfect time to trip Him up. But Jesus refused to give in to Satan's onslaught of enticing possibilities. Don't kid yourself by thinking Jesus *couldn't* sin. If He hadn't had the potential to sin, He would not have the authority to save us through His death.

Jesus was full of the Holy Spirit throughout the entire ordeal. The Spirit led Him into the wilderness and when He walked away from the tempter to begin His ministry, He did it in the power of the Holy Spirit. No one ever overflowed with the Holy Spirit as much as Jesus.

Say, "Overflow!"

4

Jesus' Disciples

Early in His ministry, Jesus selected twelve men who would become His closest companions and devoted followers. They didn't waver when He invited them to give up what they were doing and go with Him.

Put yourself in the pages of the Bible and imagine what it was like to be one of those who spent three years with Jesus. Do you think you would always be victorious? Would you say and do the right thing all the time? Does your life overflow with divine energy?

If that's the picture you see, you probably need to take another look at the Gospels. The disciples were painfully normal. Peter had a bad habit of saying and doing the wrong things. He embarrassed himself more than once (Matthew 16:21-22, 17:4-5). James and John allowed their sweet Jewish momma to ask Jesus for special favors when they got to heaven (Matthew 20:20-21). Philip proved how little he understood when he said to Jesus, "Show us the Father and it is sufficient" (John 14:8). Thomas got a bad rap because he didn't believe Jesus could possibly be alive again after His crucifixion (John 20:25). Just before Jesus was betrayed and arrested, while He agonized over what He knew was ahead, all the disciples fell asleep (Mark 14:32-41).

These were the men Jesus chose to work with. They were ordinary guys who sometimes made mistakes even though they were close friends with the King of kings.

They went everywhere with Jesus. They witnessed His compassion as He responded to people's needs. They heard Him talk—sometimes to huge crowds, other times to one person. Imagine sitting at the same table for meals, sharing your boat so He could cross a lake, or praying with Him. Can you even begin to comprehend His love, bundled together with unmatched power and wisdom?

The disciples' lives were completely wrapped up in Jesus while He taught and traveled and touched thousands of needy people. These twelve men learned to trust Him, and they believed He was the Son of God—the Messiah.

But nothing worked out the way they expected. Even though He continually tried to prepare them, they had their own ideas about His future.

The Helper is Coming!

Look at what Jesus told His followers about the Holy Spirit. The Gospel of John tells us He said:

> "These things I have spoken to you while being present with you. But the Helper, the Holy Spirit, whom the Father will send in My name, He will teach you all things, and bring to your remembrance all things that I said to you" (John 14:25-26).

That's an incredible statement. Jesus talked in depth to His disciples about the Kingdom of God, and in this Scripture He showed them what was required in order to follow His example. He promised them the Holy Spirit would teach them everything they needed to know and remind them of what Jesus Himself taught.

The disciples didn't realize how much they would have to depend on the power of the Holy Spirit, but Jesus did. And He knew they needed plenty of assurance. He understood exactly how the Holy Spirit would equip them for the work God planned for them to do as witnesses. The Holy Spirit would be vital—their Helper through the inevitable trials, temptations, and crucial decisions of their lives.

A little later, Jesus continued:

> "But when the Helper comes, whom I shall send to you from the Father, the Spirit of truth who proceeds from the Father, He will testify of Me. And you also will bear witness, because you have been with Me from the beginning" (John 15:26-27).

Jesus wanted His disciples to be ready for life after the cross, when He wouldn't be able to walk around with them in the flesh. And He repeatedly talked about the Helper who would come when He was gone. Even though these men had been with Him all along, Jesus knew they would need supernatural help to effectively communicate the Good News.

You're Leaving?

Right after that, Jesus said something the disciples couldn't begin to comprehend:

> "Nevertheless I tell you the truth. It is to your advantage that I go away; for if I do not go away, the Helper will not come to you; but if I depart, I will send Him to you" (John 16:7).

Think about how weird that must have sounded. The disciples didn't want to hear Jesus say He planned to leave! How could that possibly be good? These men were more than just buddies who did a lot of fun stuff together. They were sold-out to Jesus— completely committed to Him. Some gave up their careers. We know Levi had been a tax collector. Peter, Andrew, James, and John were all fishermen who walked away from their boats—their way of earning a living—when they met Jesus. But after spending so much time with them, He needed to convince them it would be to their advantage for Him to go away.

While He lived on earth, Jesus took on human limitations. He had to sleep, eat, and breathe just like everybody else. He could only be in one place at a time. It was essential for the disciples to understand that He had to go away before the Helper could come. Only then would the Holy Spirit—the Helper—be available to every believer, all over the globe, all the time, all through the ages. He is here for us today in whatever trials or adventures we go through. He guides us into the things God intends for us to do and empowers us to accomplish them.

Jesus knew from the start what His followers needed to complete the work the Father prepared for them. Jesus understood God's perfect plan to send the Holy Spirit. And He tried to persuade His disciples that it was good for Him to go away so the Helper could come and empower them. They were ordinary people. They needed to believe that the Holy Spirit would take over when Jesus left. He would fill them and be with them all the time. He would empower them and remind them of the things the Lord Jesus did and said. Only then would they be completely equipped to be His witnesses—ready for any situation.

That's Not What We Want!

The idea that Jesus was going to leave didn't line up with the disciples' expectations at all. The Hebrew mindset at that time was that when the Messiah came, He would overthrow Rome and usher in the long-awaited kingdom of God on earth. Right then! The disciples had high hopes for Jesus. They looked for a military victory and didn't understand that the kingdom He talked about was growing in their own hearts.

If I were one of Jesus' disciples I'd probably try to figure out how He planned to start His revolution. I might assume He could begin by winning the hearts of people, but that would only be the first step. That seems to be the view of His disciples while He was with them.

For Jesus to say He would go away without finishing what they anticipated—and that it would be for their benefit—totally baffled them. They couldn't grasp how the Holy Spirit would fill, and even overflow, from them to help them live victoriously and minister to others.

I think it's amazing that none of them asked, "I don't get it. What are You talking about?" Apparently no one dared to dig deep enough to discover what was really in Jesus' heart. They just kept thinking what they were thinking.

In spite of their confusion, it must have been awesome to be among that select group of twelve who followed Jesus. Think about it—He was large and in charge! Demons obeyed Him. Diseases lost their power in His presence. Storms dissipated at His command. He even made dead bodies alive again and fed thousands from one little boy's lunch.

While Jesus was on earth as a human being, His disciples depended on Him. He proved over and over that He could take care of any problem. They were used to being with Him and didn't want to consider the idea that He might abandon them.

Jesus drew a crowd wherever He went. People wanted to be close enough to hear every word, and maybe even touch Him. His best friends might have let their pride get a little puffed-up, because they probably inspired some awe just by being with Jesus. So when He told them it would be good for them when He left, they couldn't get beyond wondering, *but if You leave, what happens to us?*

I can almost hear Jesus saying to His disciples, "Hey, don't be discouraged. The game isn't over. It's about to get *good*."

Say, "Overflow!"

5

Jesus: God in the Flesh

The Gospels tell us Jesus was crucified like a common criminal. His trial was a sham. Before His crucifixion Roman soldiers treated Him with total contempt. They flogged Him, using a whip with sharp metal pieces attached to leather strips until the flesh on His back was shredded. They draped a purple robe around His bloodied shoulders and taunted: "Hail, King of the Jews." They hit him, spit in His face, and twisted thorny twigs into a crown that pierced His scalp when they jammed it on His head. He experienced excruciating torture even before they pounded the spikes into His hands and feet to nail Him to the cross.

Some of His followers watched—from a safe distance. They saw the indescribable agony Jesus endured, but they were too frightened to even admit they knew Him, much less try to intervene.

While Jesus hung on the cross in unbearable anguish, He cried out, "Father, forgive them; they don't know what they're doing" (Luke 23:34 MSG). You may have heard that prayer so many times you hardly think about it. But don't just read it without letting the impact sink in. He forgave the very men who tortured and finally crucified Him. How could anyone do that?

Incredible things happened while Jesus was on the cross. Darkness shrouded the land for several hours in the middle of the day. An earthquake shook buildings and even broke open a few tombs. Finally, the veil that separated the Holy of Holies from the rest of the temple was supernaturally ripped from top to bottom.

But in spite of those unexplainable phenomena, Jesus died. He was buried in a borrowed tomb.

The disciples were devastated.

He's Alive!

Even though Jesus tried and tried before that horrendous day to prepare the disciples for what was coming, when they faced the reality of His death, their hopes were crushed. On the Sunday morning after He died, these great men of faith didn't believe a few women who went to the tomb and discovered it was empty. Angels told them Jesus was alive, and they ran back to share that amazing news. Luke 24:11 says the disciples thought it sounded crazy. Everything happened exactly the way Jesus said it would, but they had to see Him themselves before they could accept the truth of His resurrection.

During the next forty days Jesus showed up in unexpected places. One time, the disciples were in a locked room, hiding from the angry Jewish leaders, and suddenly Jesus appeared right there with them. He pointed out the nail holes in His hands and the place where a soldier's spear had pierced His side (John 20:19-20).

Another incident is described in Luke 24:13-32. Jesus joined two of His followers as they walked along a road, talking about everything that had happened. The men thought He was a stranger who didn't know what had been going on. They said, "We were hoping it was He who was going to redeem Israel." At that point, the Stranger began to explain how He was revealed in the Scriptures, but they didn't recognize Him until they stopped for a meal. As soon as He blessed a loaf of bread and handed some to them, they realized it was Jesus. Then He vanished.

Jesus' followers were almost getting used to having Him with them again when He was taken up into heaven while they watched. That moment, described in Mark 16:19, Luke 24:51, and Acts 1:9, was surely the most astonishing event they ever witnessed. But it didn't change the fact that Jesus was gone. They felt like they were on their own. Again.

How did the disciples cope? We know they wrestled with uncertainty and fear. Maybe more like absolute terror. They may have had nightmares of angry soldiers—the same men who hated Jesus—

coming after them with clubs and swords. Who would be the next target?

Jesus' Final Words

The very last thing Jesus said before He ascended into heaven is recorded in Acts 1:4-8:

> And being assembled together with them, He commanded them not to depart from Jerusalem, but to wait for the Promise of the Father, "which," He said, "you have heard from Me; for John truly baptized with water, but you shall be baptized with the Holy Spirit not many days from now." Therefore, when they had come together, they asked Him, saying, "Lord, will You at this time restore the kingdom to Israel?" And He said to them, "It is not for you to know times or seasons which the Father has put in His own authority. But you shall receive power when the Holy Spirit has come upon you; and you shall be witnesses to Me in Jerusalem, and in all Judea and Samaria, and to the end of the earth."

Remember, these were the final instructions Jesus spoke to His disciples, immediately before He was taken up into heaven. Obviously, this was a crucial message—something they needed to hang onto.

When we casually talk to friends we can spend a lot of time and words that don't have any lasting impact. "Hey, how 'bout that game last night!" Or, "Boy, my grass is so brown from this heat it'll probably never come back." You know what I mean.

But I've talked to people who knew they were

close to death. They frequently have an intense desire to pass on wisdom or to help the people they love face what's ahead. There's a sense of urgency, and they choose their words carefully. A person's last remarks go deep and are usually significant.

In an even more profound way, we can be certain that this closing statement from Jesus was vitally important.

What were His instructions? "He commanded them not to depart from Jerusalem, but to wait for the Promise of the Father."

What did He say they would receive? "You will receive power...and you will be witnesses to Me in Jerusalem, and all Judea and Samaria, and to the end of the earth."

When would they receive it? "When the Holy Spirit has come upon you."

Though they surely realized this was an essential message, the disciples still got sidetracked. Look again at their response in Acts 1:6. "Lord, will You at this time restore the kingdom to Israel?" It was kind of like, "You gonna do it now, Lord? Hit Caesar in the teeth? Take over Rome and all that?"

Jesus didn't lose His patience. He just tried to refocus them. "Don't worry about those things, guys. That's the Father's business. You need to concentrate on what I want you to do for Me through the power of the Holy Spirit."

They were earthly-minded and didn't comprehend a lot of what the prophets declared or the things Jesus told them. Like you and me, sometimes they looked through a screen of their own small ideas that kept them from seeing the real picture. We can all have our minds so set in one direction that it's tough to get beyond our own expectations. Looking at Scripture from this side of Pentecost, we comprehend more of what Jesus meant, but we can empathize with the disciples. There are still a lot of things we can't figure out. One day we may look back and say, "Wow, I sure didn't understand that."

Say, "Overflow!"

6

A Promise Fulfilled

The disciples were with Jesus when He was taken up into heaven. One minute He was talking to them. The next He was gone—lifted up into the clouds.

Acts 1:9 describes it:

> Now when He had spoken these things, while they watched, He was taken up, and a cloud received Him out of their sight.

For a few moments everyone simply gazed at the empty sky, trying to figure out what happened. I understand that. What they just witnessed was beyond mind-boggling. It took some time to try to grasp what they saw.

Suddenly, two men dressed in white seemed to appear out of nowhere and spoke to them:

> "Men of Galilee," they said, "why are you standing here staring into heaven? Jesus has been taken from you into heaven, but someday He will return from heaven in the same way you saw Him go!" (Acts 1:11 NLT).

Experiencing an angelic visit could have left them even more muddled. I wonder if anyone asked the angels any questions, or if they were completely speechless. The Bible says they went back to Jerusalem, about half a mile away. But surely as they walked, their conversation must have centered on what they just watched.

Acts 1:12-14 tells us:

> Then they returned to Jerusalem from the mount called Olivet, which is near Jerusalem, a Sabbath day's journey. And when they had entered, they went up into the upper room where they were staying: Peter, James, John, and Andrew; Philip and Thomas; Bartholomew and Matthew; James the son of Alphaeus and Simon the Zealot; and Judas the son of James. These all continued with one accord in prayer and supplication, with the women and Mary the mother of Jesus, and with His brothers.

Throughout His time with them, Jesus showed His followers a new perspective on life and revealed how the values of God's kingdom apply to absolutely everything. He gave them a mission, but to accomplish it they needed the power of the Holy Spirit—the Helper. Over and over the Lord referred to the Helper He would send, but until Jesus was no longer physically with them, they probably couldn't comprehend why they might need any help.

The Promise…The Wait…The Transformation

As we've seen, the disciples were noted for thinking of themselves first. They may have felt abandoned after Jesus ascended into heaven. Possibly they wondered what would happen to them and their families. There might have been a sense of helplessness—nothing happened the way they expected. Everything seemed out of control. They surely wrestled with overwhelming emotions.

But that was before the Holy Spirit was poured out on the Day of Pentecost. Starting at that point, these very human beings began to overflow with the presence and power of God's Spirit.

Look again at what Jesus said when they were all together, immediately before He was taken into heaven:

> He commanded them not to depart from Jerusalem, but to wait for the Promise of the Father, "which," He said, "you have heard from Me; for John truly baptized with water, but you shall be baptized with the Holy Spirit not many days from now" (Acts 1:4-5).

Aren't you glad they obeyed Jesus' instructions? In spite of their questions, misgivings, and anxiety, they stayed in Jerusalem and waited. They didn't know what to expect or when, but while they waited, they prayed together. That's the very best thing we can do, especially when we're not sure what God has planned.

Look at the events that transformed them, described in Acts 2:1-4:

> When the Day of Pentecost had fully come, they were all with one accord in one place. And suddenly there came a sound from heaven, as of a rushing mighty wind, and it filled the whole house where they were sitting. Then there appeared to them divided tongues, as of fire, and one sat upon each of them. And they were all filled with the Holy Spirit and began to speak with other tongues, as the Spirit gave them utterance.

Amazing! On the Day of Pentecost, the Holy Spirit instantly transformed that frightened assembly into the strong men and women of God we think of when we read the New Testament. They finally realized how powerless they were without supernatural help. Jesus filled them with the Holy Spirit. Joy and peace and confident hope overflowed from each of the people who waited in that upper room. Their lives were forever changed when they received the power of the supernatural Helper from heaven.

And the remarkable truth is that you and I can overflow the same way, right now in the twenty-first century. We still need His supernatural power.

I believe a clear understanding of the gift of the Holy Spirit is the key to unlock the door to victory, wisdom, and power. We can experience the joyous, overflowing life every believer craves.

Depending on a Helper

I learned the advantage of having a helper—someone who would be *there* for me—when I was about ten years old. A neighborhood bully in junior high was out to get me because his girlfriend thought I was cute. He was tall and burly and way bigger than me. And he was mean.

I was by myself at a local celebration that had all sorts of entertainment—a parade, carnival rides, and concessions. I'd bought a cherry Slurpee, when this junior high dude came along with a few of his buddies and cornered me. He looked at my drink and before I had time to react, he smacked the bottom of the cup. Sticky red juice gushed all over my face and dribbled onto my clothes. I smarted-off, and he punched me in the nose, knocked me down, kicked dirt on me, then booted me a few times to finish me off. While I was on the ground, he and his cohorts took off, laughing. I was a mess, but I jumped on my bike and pedaled toward my neighborhood as fast as I could. I ended up at my best friend's house.

My friend's big brother, Ronnie, came home right after I got there. He was on the high school football team. As you can imagine, he made that junior high bully look like a little kid. When he saw me with cherry juice, blood, and dirt all over my T-shirt, he asked, "What happened to you?"

I told him what the guy did, and Ronnie marched

off, with me in his shadow, to take care of things. I thought it was really cool when we found the kid. Ronnie towered over him like a professional wrestler. He stuck out his chest, looked him right in the eye and snarled, "You ever mess with my brother again and you'll deal with me!"

After that I never had any trouble from those guys. It didn't matter that Ronnie wasn't really my brother. The troublemakers didn't know that, but they did know Ronnie could whip them without trying very hard. From then on, it was like Ronnie was right by my side all the time. Those junior high guys were afraid of me because I had power backing me up.

I'm not comparing Ronnie to the Holy Spirit except that he was available when I needed help, and that was just about as good as having him with me all the time. It gave me confidence, knowing the kids were afraid of him and he had taken up my cause.

The Holy Spirit is, in fact, a powerful ally, our supernatural Helper. He is *always* there for us. And He's so much greater than any enemy!

He's our Helper when we want to talk to people about Jesus but just can't find the right words. He helps us pray, even if we aren't sure of the situation. He strengthens us to say "no" to temptation. He gives us wisdom and discernment to make right choices. The more we depend on the Holy Spirit, the more we overflow with peace and joy and confident hope.

Say, "Overflow!"

7

The Upheaval of History

Jesus' death and resurrection changed history. Not just church history, but the entire stretch of world history. It was the most dynamic event of all time. No doubt about it.

I believe that first power-packed Pentecost is probably the second most important event in the history of the world. An extraordinary miracle started that day, and it continues to transform people all over the world. If those early believers hadn't received God's gift of the Holy Spirit, the church would not have survived. Because of supernatural help it did so much more than merely survive. The church thrived and grew and expanded for more than 2,000 years and it's still vitally alive today.

The Holy Spirit changes ordinary people into powerful witnesses who testify about the life, death, and resurrection of Jesus. They show others how Jesus is revealed throughout the Scriptures, beginning with Genesis. They tell about the amazing work He does in their own lives. And through His power, they understand the needs of those around them in order to minister effectively.

Because of the Holy Spirit, lives are transformed. Because of the Holy Spirit, every day can be an exciting adventure as we overflow with confident hope. Because of the Holy Spirit, we are never alone. Because of the Holy Spirit, we are able to follow God's plan instead of our sinful nature.

> There is therefore now no condemnation to those who are in Christ Jesus, who do not walk according to the flesh, but according to the Spirit. For the law of the Spirit of life in Christ Jesus has made me free from the law of sin and death. For what the law could not do in that it was weak through the flesh, God did by sending His own Son in the likeness of sinful flesh, on account of sin: He condemned sin in the flesh, that the righteous requirement of the law might be fulfilled in us who do not walk according to the flesh but according to the Spirit. For those who live according to the flesh set their minds on the things of the flesh, but those who live according to the Spirit, the things of the Spirit (Romans 8:1-5).

In other words, when we let the Holy Spirit lead, we can choose to obey God rather than caving in to our own desires when they don't line up with His.

The Holy Spirit is an incredible Helper!

Our Holy Coach

The Greek word for "Helper" is *paraclete*. It means one who comes alongside to help, to aid, to guide, and to teach. When I think about that, I'm reminded of a coach. Good coaches help us excel and can affect our attitudes for a long time. They motivate, encourage, and train us; we can gain so much more from them than simply strategies or techniques.

One of the first things we'd better understand when we have a coach is that if we want to improve, we have to pay attention. He knows what he's doing, and we need to learn as much as possible. If we daydream while our coach explains things, and don't practice what he teaches, we'll spend the season on the bench, or maybe not even be part of the team.

Lots of young kids don't have a clue about what to expect the first time they go out for a sport—baseball, soccer, football, whatever. Coaches have to teach some basic principles, like how to play as a team. They train young players to concentrate on the game instead of getting distracted by a rabbit that runs across the field or someone flying a kite nearby.

Maybe you weren't into sports, but you may have had a dance coach that taught proper steps and form, or a voice coach that helped you achieve a higher level of excellence. Whether it's sports or drama or music, a conscientious coach tries to help us reach our potential.

My grandpa was the first coach I ever had. When I was six years old, my dad was sent to prison. Mom wanted to be near her parents, so we drove from California to Kansas to stay with them. That was probably the best thing that could have happened to me. Grandpa had a great work ethic and strong principles.

But when we moved in with them, my grandpa had a rude awakening. I was totally ignorant about baseball. Grandpa couldn't imagine an American boy who didn't know anything about his favorite sport, so he set out to educate me. We listened to play-by-play accounts on the radio, but I couldn't visualize the game. So, Grandpa drew a baseball diamond to illustrate how it worked and we watched major league games on TV. Then he took me out to his backyard to show me how to throw and catch and bat. It didn't take too long for me to understand, and as soon as I did, I wanted to play the game.

Grandpa signed me up for little league softball, and before long I fell in love with that and just about every other sport. I wanted to try everything, and that put me in contact with more coaches. Some of those men went way beyond what anybody might expect. They made a huge impact on this fatherless kid.

I especially remember my first football coach. I didn't know anything about football—not even what equipment I needed—so I showed up for the first practice about half-dressed. I felt stupid. The coach told us what we had to get, but he knew I was from a single-parent home and must have realized that money was tight for us.

After practice he said, "I'll find some football

equipment for you." He got me a uniform with the pads and helmet and everything. He didn't make a big deal of it. He just helped a kid who wanted to play the game. Without his help, I'd have been a spectator, watching from the bleachers, wishing I could participate.

We Need the Helper

The Holy Spirit is so much more than any human coach it's beyond our comprehension. But like a coach, He comes alongside to help, to teach, and to equip us so we're ready for the next adventure. He is available all the time and knows exactly what we need. The Holy Spirit reminds us of the things Jesus taught and invites us into an intimate relationship with the King of the universe. He opens our minds to understand God's Word and prepares us to accomplish the work we're to do.

Part of that work, for every one of us, is to talk to other people about who Jesus is and what He does in our lives. That doesn't mean everyone is to preach at crusades or head for Africa to share the gospel with some remote people group. The way we act within our families, our communities, and at our jobs everyday is a loud statement to people around us. It can be a powerful witness about what the Lord is doing and how He is changing us. That power comes from relying on the Holy Spirit, rather than our own natural abilities or personalities.

I depend on the Holy Spirit every day to help me become the person God wants me to be. Even though my father wasn't a great role model, I'm not doomed to follow the same path. The Holy Spirit is teaching me how to be a loving husband, a nurturing dad, a diligent worker, and a good neighbor. His power is available all the time, to lead me so my life will be a witness to others of His amazing power. With His guidance, I can overflow every day.

Say, "Overflow!"

8

The Promise of the Father

As we've seen, it didn't take long after Jesus died for the disciples to realize they weren't going to make much of an impact on their own. Even though He still surprised them by showing up frequently after His resurrection, they didn't seem to have much purpose. John 21 tells us about one day when Peter decided to go back to his former job, fishing, and a few others joined him.

Without the Holy Spirit to motivate and empower them, they might have ultimately reverted to their old way of life. The fantastic miracles Jesus performed could have eventually slipped into forgotten history.

But God already had a plan to make sure that didn't happen. We've read parts of Acts 2 before, but check this out:

> On the day of Pentecost all the believers were meeting together in one place. Suddenly, there was a sound from heaven like the roaring of a mighty windstorm, and it filled the house where they were sitting. Then, what looked like flames or tongues of fire appeared and settled on each of them. And everyone present was filled with the Holy Spirit and began speaking in other languages, as the Holy Spirit gave them this ability. At that time there were devout Jews from every nation living in Jerusalem. When they heard the loud noise, everyone came running, and they were bewildered to hear their own languages being spoken by the believers. They were completely amazed. "How can this be?" they exclaimed. "These people are all from Galilee, and yet we hear them speaking in our own native languages!" (Acts 2:1-8 NLT).

In spite of being worried and disillusioned, about 120 believers clustered together for prayer, waiting for the Promise of the Father, which Jesus predicted (Luke 24:49). They didn't know what to expect, but they obeyed His command to wait in Jerusalem. The disciples were there, along with dozens of other men and women, including Jesus' mother and brothers. They met together daily, but that day—Pentecost— what started as a quiet prayer meeting didn't stay that way. They must have gotten pretty rowdy to attract so much attention.

Jerusalem was packed with Jews who came from all over the region to celebrate the traditional Hebrew festival of Pentecost. But everybody stopped what they were doing to find out what was going on. Above the general din of a big crowd, they heard a powerful wind and the voices of over a hundred people praising God in different languages. If we were on the outside looking into that room and saw what happened, with no New Testament to refer to, what would we think?

Honestly, it's kind of freaky! A noise, like a strong wind, swirls through the room, even though the sun is shining and the weather is calm. Flames hover over the heads of all the people, but they aren't burned. Instead, a new passion is ignited within them. The whole group is filled with the Holy Spirit and they instantly become bold, no longer shrinking in fear. They begin to speak in other languages, so that all the different people hear God being praised in their own mother-tongues.

Wow!

Some hecklers in the crowd tried to blow it off, "Don't pay any attention—they're just drunk." (Acts 2:13). That cracks me up. I've seen plenty of drunks, and believe me, being inebriated doesn't improve anyone's linguistic skills. You have to be careful when you're speaking some languages. A little nuance or subtle tone change can make a big difference in the meaning of certain words. People can't manage a foreign language well if their minds are fuzzy from too much wine.

Maybe the disciples seemed intoxicated because

they were so ecstatic over what happened that they lost some natural inhibitions and weren't concerned about their dignity.

Most of the people milling around Jerusalem were probably stunned by what they saw and heard. Imagine how some may have talked about it with each other.

"What do you suppose is going on?"

"Beats me! They're talking about the awesome works of God."

"Hey, listen. These people are all speaking different languages!"

"Some of them are talking in my dialect, but aren't they all locals?"

Think about it. This was a group of native Galileans, all telling the same message in languages from every area of the known world. These newly Spirit-filled believers weren't scholars. They had varied backgrounds, including fishermen, carpenters or other tradesmen, and one was a tax collector before he met Jesus. Some were probably loyal to Rome and others diametrically opposed. They were definitely a rag-tag, diverse mix. Some may have been well educated, but overall this was no world-class church-planting team. It was just a group of regular people like you and me.

Can you see why Jesus called the Holy Spirit the Helper? He certainly helped them do something they never could have managed on their own.

But remember, this was just the *beginning* of what Jesus called "the Promise of My Father." Everything changed from that point forward. The power of God became available to all believers—ordinary men and women—like never before. The new church was empowered that day to be witnesses who would testify to the world what they knew about the Lord. They overflowed with confident hope through the power of the Holy Spirit.

Peter: From Coward to Confident

At Jesus' trial a few weeks earlier, Peter trembled with fear as he mingled with the guards and servants who warmed themselves by a fire. Three times that night, he denied he even knew Jesus (Luke 22:54-62).

But through the life-changing experience of the baptism in the Holy Spirit, Peter became so confident that he saw the mocking throng as an audience that needed to hear the truth. Peter had never been meek or quiet, but that day he received a holy boldness to testify about the Lord Jesus. Peter's words were full of wisdom, rooted in Scripture instead of some of the off-the-wall statements he was noted for prior to Pentecost. Think about the things he said as he overflowed with power from the Holy Spirit.

First, Peter explained that none of them were drunk—after all, it was only about nine o'clock in the morning. He announced to the crowd that what they saw and heard that day was the amazing fulfillment of ancient prophecies. Then he went on to quote the prophet Joel, saying:

> "'In the last days,' God says, 'I will pour out my Spirit upon all people. Your sons and daughters will prophesy, your young men will see visions, and your old men will dream dreams. In those days I will pour out my Spirit even on my servants—men and women alike—and they will prophesy. But everyone

who calls on the name of the LORD will be saved'" (Acts 2:17, 18, 21 NLT).

Next, Peter zeroed in on their problem, and like a boxer's powerful blow, it left them reeling:

> "But God knew what would happen, and his prearranged plan was carried out when Jesus was betrayed. With the help of lawless Gentiles, you nailed him to the cross and killed him. But God released him from the horrors of death and raised him back to life, for death could not keep him in its grip" (Acts 2:23-24 NLT).

Some of the listeners realized they really were guilty of murder. They had murdered the Son of God, the Messiah! Those whose hearts were pierced asked Peter and the other apostles, "Brothers, now what do we do?"

In the first of what would become many powerful messages, Peter explained exactly what they had to do to be saved:

> "Repent, and let every one of you be baptized in the name of Jesus Christ for the remission of sins; and you shall receive the gift of the Holy Spirit" (Acts 2:38).

Notice that Peter assured them that everyone who repented and trusted Jesus as Savior would be forgiven. No question about it. Some of these people may have been in the mob that shouted, "Crucify Him!" when Pilate wanted to set Jesus free. But nothing in their past kept God's love and grace from those who turned to Him. And that is still true today.

Peter didn't say they *might* receive the gift of the Holy Spirit, or that only *some* of them would. It was a promised gift for everyone who put their trust in Christ. That very day about 3,000 people repented. They gave their lives to Jesus and He filled them with the Holy Spirit. From that moment on, they were eternally changed.

What a power-packed day! Probably the most spectacular miracle was that the presence of the Holy Spirit transformed this group of average, anxious people into bold men and women, full of wisdom and authority. They overflowed with confident hope through the power of the Holy Spirit and worked together to share the gospel message.

Christians all believe the account of what happened that day. Why wouldn't we? It's right there in Scripture! But there are things some people struggle with and even disagree about. Who is the gift of the Holy Spirit for? When do we receive the gift? What does it mean to us? How do we receive the baptism in the Holy Spirit?

In the next chapters we'll look at these questions one by one and see what the Bible says.

Say, "Overflow!"

9

Who Is the Gift of the Holy Spirit For?

Some people say the baptism in the Holy Spirit was a special gift only for the disciples. But it's clear in the book of Acts that countless people received it long after that first outpouring.

Certain denominations believe it was for the early church and it isn't available for us today. They assume the gifts were just for that time, and somehow they've passed away.

Others think people get the Holy Spirit when they're born again, but that the spiritual gifts don't exist anymore. They believe we receive everything we will ever get from God when we repent and pray for salvation.

A few groups go to the other extreme and make the baptism in the Holy Spirit their primary focus. They imply that no one is really saved without it.

In my opinion, these views all contradict Scripture and put weird limits on the ministry of God's Spirit in our generation.

Check the Word of God

When I'm given a choice between man's traditions or God's Word, I go with the Word every time. Look again at the end of Peter's compelling message in Acts 2:38:

> "Repent, and let every one of you be baptized in the name of the Lord Jesus Christ for the remission of sins; and you shall receive the gift of the Holy Spirit."

I see three major points here:

1. Repentance—turn from sin to follow Jesus
2. Water baptism—an outward expression of an inward change
3. The gift of the Holy Spirit—God's empowering presence

Would any Christian say that repentance is no longer necessary? Or that water baptism is outdated? If not, how could anyone believe that only two of these three things are still relevant today?

Do you think God wants us to pick and choose? "Okay kids, if some Scriptures make you uncomfortable, you don't have to believe them. Take what sounds good and just ignore the rest of your Bible."

Does that make any sense?

This isn't a buffet where we can select what we want and bypass the rest. When I go to a buffet, I know what I want, and what I don't. I won't put anything on my plate that doesn't appeal to me. But it's scary to think that some people do that with God's Word. They believe His promises about salvation, but disregard what He says about the baptism in the Holy Spirit.

The Bible is God's living Word. Will you believe it or not? As a teacher of God's Word, I take my responsibility very seriously, and I'm grieved when people ignore Scriptures that don't fit their theology.

We've Been Called

Acts 2:39 specifies who this promise is for:

> "For the promise is to you and to your children, and to all who are afar off, as many as the Lord our God will call."

This short scripture is packed with reassurance for everyone who follows Jesus. First, Peter told them God promised the gift of the Holy Spirit to those who were right there listening to him speak. And the promise is to their children, pointing to future generations. Then he included those who were far off, so it wasn't limited to Jerusalem or even the various nationalities represented in the city that day. Finally, it was for as many as the Lord God calls. That gathers in every believer, and there's no expiration date on the Bible.

We've all been called. Jesus reminds us in Luke 5:32, "I have not come to call the righteous, but sinners, to repentance."

In 1 Peter 2:9 we're told:

> But you are a chosen generation, a royal priesthood, a holy nation, His own special people, that you may proclaim the praises of Him who called you out of darkness into His marvelous light.

And Ephesians 4:4 says:

> There is one body and one Spirit, just as you were called in one hope of your calling.

Finally, Paul assures Timothy, and us:

> ...[God] has saved us and called us with a holy calling, not according to our works, but according to His own purpose and grace which was given to us in Christ Jesus before time began (2 Timothy 1:9).

If this gift is for the people God calls, or chooses, don't you suppose it includes you and me and every other believer throughout every generation? Nobody is left out.

So there shouldn't be any question about it. This gift is for all Christians, in all nations, through all ages. God knew, way before that first outpouring of the Holy Spirit, that we would need to be empowered just as much in the twenty-first century as they did in the first. Why? Remember what's recorded in Acts 1:8. Jesus said:

> "But you shall receive power when the Holy Spirit has come upon you; and you shall be witnesses to Me in Jerusalem, and in all Judea and Samaria, and to the end of the earth."

Clearly, He expects us to be witnesses, telling others about Him. Do you feel capable of doing that on your own? I don't. Thank goodness, He doesn't ask us to represent Him in isolation.

A Witness Testifies

Think about what it means to be a witness. Have you ever witnessed a crime or an accident? I did, on my way home from the airport one evening after a powerful leadership conference. As I waited at a red light, my mind wandered somewhere else. I was thinking about things I learned at the meetings I attended, and about getting home to my family. All of a sudden . . . wham! Two vehicles collided right in front of me. I jumped out of my car to make sure everybody was okay, while someone else dialed 911.

One of the police officers who responded asked, "Did you witness the accident?"

"Uh, yeah . . . I guess." I tried to remember what I just saw. *Let's see, he hit her I think. But did she run a red light?* It happened right in front of me, but I hadn't been paying close attention. I told the officer as much as I could piece together.

Later I was summoned to court to testify. Fortunately, there were other witnesses who had been more focused and gave clear accounts of the accident. I remember thinking, *I'm so glad they can testify about what they saw.*

Testify. That's what a witness does, and what we're supposed to do as believers. We tell people what we know about Jesus and the kingdom of heaven. We talk about what we've seen and experienced as the Lord moved in our own lives. Because God knows us, He doesn't expect us to do a great job on our own. Without the power of the Holy Spirit, our testimony is ineffective, like mine after the accident.

When we overflow with the power of the Holy Spirit, not only do we know what to share, we can depend on Him to direct our words. That's why the baptism in the Holy Spirit is essential if we want to lead a victorious life and help others get to know Jesus for themselves.

Sometimes the Holy Spirit brings a particular Scripture to mind that is precisely right for that situation. Or He may give us knowledge about some aspect of a person's life that needs to be addressed. God is familiar with everything about each individual, and His ideas on how to reach us are unlimited.

We Need Power

Going back to the original question: Who is the baptism in the Holy Spirit for? Obviously, it is for everyone who needs supernatural power to be a good witness.

And who needs it?

Who doesn't!

Jesus said in John 14:16-17:

"And I will pray the Father, and He will give you another Helper, that He may abide with you forever—the Spirit of truth, whom the world cannot receive, because it neither sees Him nor knows Him; but you know Him, for He dwells with you and will be in you."

It's clear, Jesus was talking to believers—those who trusted in Him and were already convinced that He was the long-awaited Messiah. He said unbelievers *can't* receive the Holy Spirit because they don't even know Him. The only prerequisite to receiving the Holy Spirit is that we believe.

The word "believe" lacks the depth and intensity in English that the Greek word implies. We might say, "I believe I'll go shopping." Or, "Can you believe how long the preacher talked this morning?"

I've heard people say, "Sure, I believe in Jesus." But all they mean is that they acknowledge the fact that Jesus really lived and the things in the Bible actually happened. The Bible tells us even demons know that ... and they tremble (James 2:19).

In the New Testament, the word translated, "believe" is *pisteuo*. It means to trust in, rely on, cling to, and be fully convinced of. It's a statement of personal confidence that produces obedience and submission to the Lordship of Jesus.

The people Jesus talked to in John 14 were ready to receive the gift of the Holy Spirit because they trusted in Him. He hadn't filled them yet, but He promised to send the Helper, who would abide in them forever. Jesus knew they needed the power they would receive from the baptism in the Holy Spirit.

Only then could they overflow with confidence and become remarkable witnesses who would change the world.

Say, "Overflow!"

10

When Do We Receive the Holy Spirit?

Some people say that we receive the Holy Spirit at salvation, and they're absolutely right.

I love the way the *New Living Translation* puts it in 2 Corinthians 1:22:

> He has identified us as his own by placing the Holy Spirit in our hearts as the first installment that guarantees everything he has promised us.

There's no argument about whether or not the Holy Spirit comes into our hearts when we are identified as belonging to Christ. But Scripture unmistakably teaches that the *baptism* in the Holy Spirit is a separate event. You can receive it any time *after* you're born again. It may only be a few minutes later, or it might be years, but it's definitely not part of the same package. God makes it clear in the book of Acts that the baptism in the Holy Spirit isn't automatically included in salvation.

Why two experiences? I honestly don't know, but I think that's a good question. We'll have to ask God about that when we get to heaven.

Let's look at a few examples. We'll not only see that the two experiences are distinct, but these Scriptures also show the importance of the baptism of the Holy Spirit.

Going to Samaria

Check out this great story in Acts:

> Then Philip went down to the city of Samaria and preached Christ to them. And the multitudes with one accord heeded the things spoken by Philip, hearing and seeing the miracles which he did. For unclean spirits, crying with a loud voice, came out of many who were possessed; and many who were paralyzed and lame were healed. And there was great joy in that city. ... But when they believed Philip as he preached the things concerning the kingdom of God and the name of Jesus Christ, both men and women were baptized (Acts 8:5-8, 12).

Philip, one of the original twelve disciples, went on a short-term mission trip—to Samaria of all places. That may not seem like anything out of the ordinary, but because of the attitude of people at that time, it was incredible. The Jews despised the Samaritans. They saw them as second-rate citizens and didn't usually want any contact with them. Some Jewish people even skirted far out of their way to avoid traveling through Samaria. But God never draws dividing lines like that and He moves us beyond our man-made boundaries. His grace can fill our hearts with compassion for people we might not care about on our own.

I love Philip's obedience. He went beyond his comfort and culture to do what the Lord prompted him to do. He preached about Jesus and told the Samaritans amazing things concerning the kingdom of God. Philip's message was backed by the Holy Spirit's power, and the Samaritans believed. Demons came out of people, and those who were paralyzed or crippled were healed. Talk about a revival!

The Bible sometimes seems to understate things. It says there was great joy in the city. I think they celebrated. I can imagine dancing in the streets, everybody with a big grin. They probably laughed and shouted and hugged each other. They hadn't expected God to do any miracles for them—but He did! And the biggest miracle of all is that their hearts were changed. Many people believed and were water baptized. Then Philip went on his way to share the gospel with others.

When the apostles in Jerusalem heard that some Samaritans became Christians, they were probably skeptical.

"You mean God actually saved Samaritans?"

"I never heard of such a thing!"

"Do you think it's for real?"

So, they sent Peter and John to find out exactly what happened. Peter and John were the big guys! They'd been tight with Jesus. They were even on the mountain with Him when Moses and Elijah came down. For the church to send those two shows how important this was.

They went to Samaria to talk to the people and discovered that many of the Samaritans really had become Christians. But the Holy Spirit had not yet "fallen" upon any of them. So Peter and John laid hands on those new converts and prayed for them to receive the Holy Spirit (Acts 8:14-17).

As a result of Philip's message, people were born again and water baptized. God healed the sick and delivered the demon-possessed through his ministry. That's a big deal! But the apostles knew the Samaritans still needed the power that comes from the baptism in the Holy Spirit. The Samaritans didn't receive that gift until Peter and John laid hands on them. It was clearly a second experience—totally separate from their salvation.

Christians in Ephesus

Another story, this one in Acts 19, tells about some believers the Apostle Paul met when he traveled to Ephesus. I'll paraphrase the story. Paul asked, "Did you receive the Holy Spirit when you believed?"

They must have looked confused and might have said, "Umm ... what do you mean? We've never even heard of the Holy Spirit."

Paul asked them, "Then what baptism did you experience?"

"We were baptized by John."

"Okay," Paul said. "John's baptism called for repentance from sin, so that's good. But John himself told people to believe in the One who would come after him, who would baptize them with the Holy Spirit. He was talking about Jesus."

Paul went on to tell them everything Jesus had done for them. As soon as they heard, they put their trust in Jesus and wanted to be water baptized in His name.

Acts 19:6 says:

> And when Paul had laid hands on them, the Holy Spirit came upon them, and they spoke with tongues and prophesied.

They must have been ecstatic, and from that moment on, they praised God in languages they had never learned, and told others about His mighty acts. They *overflowed* with confident hope.

If the baptism in the Holy Spirit automatically happens as soon as a person believes, would Peter and John have made the trip to Samaria? Would Paul have bothered to ask the Ephesians if they had received Him? These were definitely two independent events, probably separated by quite a length of time.

My Own Experience

Some people receive the baptism in the Holy Spirit just moments after they put their trust in Jesus. That's what happened to me. I had always believed in God. I knew that He existed. But I didn't *know* Him. I hadn't gone to church regularly and didn't understand anything about the Bible.

Then one Sunday I visited a church that was very motivated to move in the gifts of the Holy Spirit. I felt like an outsider, but when the pastor gave an invitation for people to turn their lives over to Jesus, I absolutely couldn't resist. God was really working on me. I was desperate for something real; no more pretending. I was only seventeen, but I felt used up and tired. That morning, I walked down the aisle to the front of that church and repented. I asked Jesus to take charge of my life. Even though I didn't know anything about being a Christian, I wanted everything the Lord had to offer.

While I stood there, the pastor's wife came over, looked in my eyes, and said, "You've been surrendering to the things of the world, and now you need to surrender your life to Jesus. There's a big hole in your heart that used to be full of sin. You just kicked the sin out, but now you need to let the Holy Spirit come in and fill you."

Then she started saying some things that made a huge impact, things she had no way of knowing. She might have picked up clues about my culture from my appearance. I had long hair, a Harley Davidson sweatshirt and biker boots, but the words she spoke to me went deeper than appearances. How did she know? She depended on the power of the Holy Spirit.

Right then, about five minutes after I gave my life to the Lord Jesus, I prayed to be baptized in the Holy Spirit. I experienced the cleansing and indwelling power of God in a way that I will never forget. Peace invaded, and replaced my confusion and pain as soon as I let Him in. No one can take that experience from me. I can't begin to describe what took place inside me at that moment. I'm not just talking about emotion; God began a total renovation of my heart— an extreme makeover!

Don't get me wrong, I didn't suddenly become a preacher. When I walked out of the church that day I was still cussing like before, but dramatic changes began happening from the inside out. It's been a process of transformation that continues to this day. The baptism in the Holy Spirit has made a huge difference in my life, and I guarantee it will in yours, too.

Okay. We see that this gift is for all believers throughout history and we can receive it any time after salvation. Let's go on to the third question.

Say, "Overflow!"

11

What Does it Mean for Us?

Why should you want the baptism in the Holy Spirit? It's easy to see that the early Christians needed it to face trials they dealt with and accomplish the work God gave them. People today need that baptism if they have a clergy sticker on their bumper or serve as missionaries in a foreign culture. But you're not in any of those roles. You just go to work every day or take care of your family or go to school. You do the things you need to do, ordinary stuff. No need for special spiritual power.

Nowhere does Scripture say that you *have* to be

baptized in the Holy Spirit or that it's a prerequisite for salvation. So what's the big deal?

That's a good question. There are lots of reasons, but I'll just mention a few here.

The Holy Spirit is Our Helper

We've already looked at Scriptures that say the Holy Spirit is the Helper, but it's important enough to emphasize again. Jesus promised supernatural help for everyone who obeys Him, and He repeatedly called the Holy Spirit a Helper.

Remember what Jesus said in John 15:26:

> "But when the Helper comes, whom I shall send to you from the Father, the Spirit of truth who proceeds from the Father, He will testify of Me."

Without help from the Holy Spirit, we come up short when we try to witness or pray for people or even live victoriously day-by-day within our families and communities.

Remember the Greek word *parakletos?* I said it means "helper" and also "one who comes alongside." Think about that.

When we open ourselves to the Holy Spirit, we know God is with us all the time, to help us through every situation we face. I don't know about you, but I need all the help I can get!

Jesus Himself depended on the Holy Spirit. In Luke, we're told He went to the synagogue and read from a scroll the prophet Isaiah wrote about 700 hundred years earlier.

"The Spirit of the Lord is upon Me, because
He has anointed Me to preach the gospel to
the poor; He has sent Me to heal the
brokenhearted, to proclaim liberty to the cap-
tives and recovery of sight to the blind, to set
at liberty those who are oppressed; to
proclaim the acceptable year of the Lord"
(Luke 4:18-19).

When He finished reading, Jesus closed the book
and said, "Today this Scripture is fulfilled in your
hearing" (verse 21). In other words, "That's Me Isaiah
was talking about! And the Holy Spirit is directing My
ministry."

If Jesus needed help from the Holy Spirit, surely
we don't think we can manage without Him!

The Holy Spirit is Our Comforter

Do you ever feel beat-up by life? *Parakletos* can
also be translated as *Comforter*.

Acts 9:31 says:

And walking in the fear of the Lord and in the
comfort of the Holy Spirit, they were
multiplied.

Paul tells us in 2 Corinthians 1:3-4:

Blessed be the God and Father of our Lord
Jesus Christ, the Father of mercies and God
of all comfort, who comforts us in all our
tribulation, that we may be able to comfort
those who are in any trouble, with the

comfort with which we ourselves are comforted by God.

I like the way the *Message* paraphrases John 14:16:

"I will talk to the Father, and He'll provide you another Friend so that you will always have someone with you."

That sounds good to me. He'll never turn on me. He will always be there when I need assurance, to remind me I'm special to God. We all need that sometimes.

The Holy Spirit is Our Teacher
Look again at Jesus' words from John 14:26:

"But the Helper, the Holy Spirit, whom the Father will send in My name, He will teach you all things, and bring to your remembrance all things that I said to you."

And in Luke 12:12, Jesus says, "For the Holy Spirit will teach you in that very hour what you ought to say."

The Holy Spirit teaches us, and I want to be a good student. He reminds us of the powerful things Jesus said. That's an awesome promise. I may not remember everything I'd like to, but the Holy Spirit does.

When I need a Bible verse to encourage or counsel someone, He can bring the best one to my mind. That doesn't mean we shouldn't study the

Word of God. But if we are obedient to read, memorize, and examine the Scriptures, He will give us the perfect words at the right time to accomplish what the Father wants. What a privilege!

The Holy Spirit is Our Guide

In John 16:13 we read:

> "When He, the Spirit of truth, has come, He will guide you into all truth; for He will not speak on His own authority, but whatever He hears He will speak."

Occasionally most of us think, *I wish someone would show me what to do.* That's exactly what Jesus said the Holy Spirit will do. He's like a divine Global Positioning System—a GPS. But instead of depending on a satellite, we're connected to God. Satellites can fail, but we never have to worry about the Holy Spirit not functioning properly. He sees where we are all the time, and He knows the next step we need to take to get where we're supposed to go.

Romans 8:14 says: "For as many as are led by the Spirit of God, these are sons of God." I can't think of a higher honor than to be called a son of God. Being led by the Holy Spirit is actually a lordship issue. The real question is: Who is directing my life? If the Holy Spirit is our leader—our guide—we are eligible to be called children of God. Awesome!

The Holy Spirit is Our Source of Power

Power is what the overflow is all about. In Acts 1:8 Jesus exhorted the disciples, as well as you and me. He said:

"You shall receive power when the Holy
Spirit has come upon you; and you shall be
witnesses to Me in Jerusalem, and in all Judea
and Samaria, and to the end of the earth."

If we struggle with the ability to witness
effectively, He offers everything we need. The Holy
Spirit gives us the power to be God's people and
fulfill our purposes. It doesn't matter if we're in
Kansas City or Los Angeles or some remote part of
the world most people haven't even heard of.

On our own, we can open our mouths and say a
bunch of words (sometimes more than we should).
But when those words are empowered by God,
through the Holy Spirit, they can pierce a cold heart
or heal a hurting one. They will accomplish whatever
He wants and precisely what that person needs.

The Holy Spirit Can Work Through Us

There is nothing like being used by God to touch
the heart of another person. I'll always remember one
of the first times I experienced a supernatural word of
wisdom from the Lord. I was serving as a youth
pastor. We had a great youth facility called Zoe House
that attracted kids who might never go to a church,
and God was doing awesome things.

One evening a college girl said, "Will you talk to
my campus group?" It was in a town about a hundred
miles away. That sounded cool.

"Sure. Let's figure out when." I wrote the date on
my calendar, and to tell the truth, I didn't think about
it again until the day I was supposed to be there.
Hmmm … Lord, what do You want me to talk about?

I was just about to leave for the college town

when a teenager came to my office with a big problem. He'd been at some of our youth meetings, but I hadn't seen much of him lately. He told me that he just found out his girlfriend was pregnant. And what was worse, her parents wanted her to have an abortion. He was unpacking all this when I glanced at my watch and realized I had to leave. I should have gone about twenty minutes earlier.

I couldn't walk out on him, so I said, "Look, I've got to go. Why don't you come with me and we'll talk on the way."

I listened to him as we drove, but I didn't have a chance to think about what to share with this college group. I had never been so totally unprepared to speak.

We got there and went in, but it didn't even seem like a Christian group. They were having fun, singing a secular song, and then the leader did a fast introduction, "We have a special speaker tonight, his name's Clint." That was it. I started to talk, but it really felt flat.

The amazing thing was that in spite of my lack of preparation, God touched some kids. Several people came to talk to me afterwards and a couple of them gave their hearts to the Lord, so I was pumped.

I was ready to go home when one girl came to me and said, "When I was younger it seemed like God called me to be a missionary and I still really want to do that." She was excited and talked about how she sensed God leading her. But the whole time we talked I was totally distracted; the word *abortion* kept going through my mind. I can't say I heard an audible voice, but it was very clear and I didn't know what to make of it.

As she walked away, the only way to describe what I felt was that it seemed like I was in sin. I began to pray, "Lord what's was going on?" He immediately showed me that I needed to go back to her.

I asked a girl from the group's leadership team to go with me, and we found the one who wanted to be a missionary. I said, "Can we talk some more? Someplace private?" She nodded. Probably figured I wanted to discuss Papua New Guinea or something.

The three of us went off to one side and I said, "I don't know why, but all the time we talked, the word *abortion* kept coming to my mind. Does that mean anything to you?"

As soon as I asked, she started to cry. I had never seen anyone so broken. She confessed that she'd had an abortion, and she was so ashamed.

I sensed the Holy Spirit's presence, and I said, "Look, what you did was a sin, but Jesus came to save sinners. Having sex when you weren't married was sin. Getting rid of your baby for your own convenience was sin. But God loves you and wants to forgive you. He'll make you whole, so the memory of what you did doesn't keep you locked in the past. You can start fresh."

She sobbed uncontrollably, and I knew God was doing a powerful work in her. The other girl put her arms around her and just held her. Eventually her tears ended and she started to laugh. Her face was all red and puffy, but she just lit up with joy as she accepted the Lord's forgiveness. She was already a believer, but that sin held her down like a heavy weight.

The girls hugged and cried and laughed together. And I knew they didn't need me any longer. I was so humbled—and so awed—to know God used me to show His heart to that girl.

That's what the power of the Holy Spirit can do. When we overflow with confident hope from the Holy Spirit, He ministers to people so much deeper than anything we can work up on our own.

By the way, let me tell you what happened with the teenager who rode along with me. We talked all the way, and by the time we got home, he made some tough decisions. He encouraged his girlfriend to go to a local Christian facility that helps unwed pregnant women. She chose to keep their baby, and they got married as soon as possible. Now they have seven kids, are active at LifeMission Church, and that first "baby" is involved in our youth ministry. Never underestimate the power of the Holy Spirit.

Say, "Overflow!"

12

How Do We Receive the Holy Spirit?

The baptism in the Holy Spirit is a gift. We can accept it or refuse.

What if somebody gave me a present, done up with fancy paper and a big bow, but all I did was admire the package and say, "Thank you." Then I put it on a shelf and never opened it. I might even point it out to friends, "Look at this beautiful package." What good would it do? It could be some tool I've wanted, or season tickets to the KU Jayhawks, or a new worship CD. But if I don't open it, I won't know.

Believe me, I've never refused to open a present. I

can't imagine saying, "No thanks, I don't really want to find out what's inside." When I receive a gift, I rip the paper off and can't wait to see what it is. That's how we should be with God. He wants us to respond to His gifts with the eager anticipation of a little kid on Christmas morning.

Let's look at what Jesus said about that in Luke 11:9-13:

> "So I say to you, ask, and it will be given to you; seek, and you will find; knock and it will be opened to you. For everyone who asks receives, and he who seeks finds, and to him who knocks it will be opened. If a son asks for bread from any father among you, will he give him a stone? Or if he asks for a fish will he give him a serpent instead of a fish? Or if he asks for an egg, will he offer him a scorpion? If you then, being evil, know how to give good gifts to your children, how much more will your heavenly Father give the Holy Spirit to those who ask Him!"

If we know the baptism in the Holy Spirit is a gift from God, how should we respond? What did you just read? "So I say to you, *ask*, and it will be given to you . . . for everyone who asks receives." It's that simple!

When the Lord offers the gift of salvation, we receive it by faith. We don't have to wait until we're good enough to earn it (whatever "good enough" means). We don't need to beg and plead or have a deep understanding of theology. It's the same with the gift of the Holy Spirit.

Go back to the last sentence of that passage. " … *how much more* will your heavenly Father give the Holy Spirit to those who ask Him!" That emphasizes the idea that Father *wants* to give us the Holy Spirit.

As parents, Mary and I love to give gifts to our kids and to know they are excited to get them. Maybe your parents didn't feel that way, but most of us have heard heartwarming stories of people who give, just for the joy their gift will bring to others. Or possibly you've been able to provide for a special need, and felt the thrill of blessing someone else. I believe it makes our heavenly Father happy when we are as eager to receive as He is to give.

The people in the upper room on Pentecost, 2,000 years ago, were just ordinary men and women. They loved Jesus and yearned for the power He promised. They were no more super-spiritual than you or me. Their desire to obey drew them together "with one accord," as it says in Acts 2:1.

They asked. He gave. They received. They did the natural. He did the supernatural.

One thing I want to make clear is that the baptism in the Holy Spirit isn't merely a feeling. Emotions come and go. Some people have a very moving experience when they receive this gift. Others don't feel anything. God works in a marvelous, personal way to meet the needs of each individual.

Let's Go Over the Basics

You may not need this reminder, but bear with me while I summarize what we've talked about so far.

John the Baptist promised that Jesus Himself would baptize us in the Holy Spirit. It's incredible to realize the Creator of the universe will saturate us till we overflow with His Spirit. In Matthew 3:11, John said:

> "I indeed baptize you with water unto repentance, but He who is coming after me is mightier than I, whose sandals I am not worthy to carry. He will baptize you with the Holy Spirit and fire."

And in John 1:33:

> "He who sent me to baptize with water said to me, 'Upon whom you see the Spirit descending, and remaining on Him, this is He who baptizes with the Holy Spirit.'"

While He lived on earth, Jesus took on the limitations of humanity, but as soon as He returned to heaven, the Holy Spirit became available to every believer. They were like a tag-team. In John 16:7, Jesus tried to convince His disciples they would be better off when He went away:

> "Nevertheless I tell you the truth. It is to your advantage that I go away; for if I do not go away, the Helper will not come to you; but if I depart, I will send Him to you."

Jesus told His followers to stay in Jerusalem until they received the Promise of the Father. This was so important, it was the very last command He gave before He was taken to heaven. Acts 1:4:

> And being assembled together with them, He
> commanded them not to depart from
> Jerusalem, but to wait for the Promise of the
> Father, "which," He said, "you have heard
> from Me."

On our own, even though we love the Lord and
want to tell people about Him, we aren't very
effective unless we depend on the power of the Holy
Spirit. He fills believers with power to witness and
minister. Look at Acts 1:8:

> "But you shall receive power when the Holy
> Spirit has come upon you; and you shall be
> witnesses to Me in Jerusalem, and in all Judea
> and Samaria, and to the end of the earth."

Jesus referred to the Holy Spirit as the Helper,
over and over. Obviously, we need all the help we can
get to become the people God created us to be and to
overflow onto those around us. When Jesus talked to
His disciples in John 14:26, He said:

> "But the Helper, the Holy Spirit, whom the
> Father will send in My name, He will teach
> you all things, and bring to your remembrance
> all things that I said to you."

The Holy Spirit will always lift up the name of
Jesus and make His presence real. We need to keep
that in mind if we ever wonder whether something is
from God's Spirit. Jesus wasn't boasting in John 15:26
when He said:

> "But when the Helper comes, whom I shall send to you from the Father, the Spirit of truth who proceeds from the Father, He will testify of Me."

Finally, the Holy Spirit reminds us of the things Jesus said, and helps us understand Scripture way beyond our own ability. Jesus assures us in John 16:13:

> "However, when He, the Spirit of truth, has come, He will guide you into all truth; for He will not speak on His own authority, but whatever He hears He will speak."

Are You Obedient?

Jesus longs for everyone who loves Him to accept the gifts He offers. If we're obedient, we want the same things He wants for us, right? Obedience is one of the basic foundation stones to build our faith upon. Those first Christians obeyed. Right before Jesus ascended into heaven He said, "Go to Jerusalem and wait for the Promise of the Father." They did what He told them to do, when He told them to do it. They went and waited.

What if they had come up with excuses? "Oh, sorry, my schedule's really packed right now. That'll have to wait till I have more time." Or maybe, "I'm just not convinced I need anything more. I believe in You, Jesus. That's enough for me."

Aren't you glad they went to Jerusalem right then and prayed together while they waited? They were eager to receive everything Jesus wanted to give. The church today is a direct result of the obedience of the people in that prayer group.

When the Lord directs His people to do something, it's because He wants to provide for them and protect them. He provided the power those first Christians needed to be good witnesses. He protected them from the failure that was sure to result if they depended on their own strength to make an impact. He wants the same thing for us. And without a doubt, we need His power and protection just as desperately as they did.

God has a vested interest in us! We can be confident that He always wants the best for us. And overflowing with power from the Holy Spirit is absolutely best.

Say, "Overflow!"

13

First Things First

I pray that your heart is stirred, and you sincerely want everything God longs to give. Without a doubt, the most important decision you will ever make—the only thing that matters for eternity—hinges on one question. Have you asked Jesus to forgive you and come into your life as Lord and Savior?

If you haven't taken that first step yet, today can be the day of your salvation. There's no better time than now. Please don't put off something so vital.

There's a fascinating story in John 3 about a Pharisee, a ruler of the Jews named Nicodemus. He probably heard Jesus speak in the temple sometimes, and believed He was sent from God. Nicodemus wanted to talk to Jesus, but was hesitant because of the other religious leaders, who were violently opposed to His teaching. Huge crowds seemed to follow Jesus everywhere, so Nicodemus waited until he could talk to Him privately, after dark, away from the mob.

Nicodemus didn't even have a chance to ask his questions before Jesus charged right into the heart of the matter. We read in John 3:3-7:

> Jesus answered and said to him, "Most assuredly, I say to you, unless one is born again, he cannot see the kingdom of God." Nicodemus said to Him, "How can a man be born when he is old? Can he enter a second time into his mother's womb and be born?" Jesus answered, "Most assuredly, I say to you, unless one is born of water and the Spirit, he cannot enter the kingdom of God. That which is born of the flesh is flesh, and that which is born of the Spirit is spirit. Do not marvel that I said to you, 'You must be born again.'"

Like everything else Jesus said, what He told Nicodemus is still true for us today. We must be born again to enter into the kingdom of God. Have you made that all-important decision?

God isn't concerned with your history—He wants you to spend your future with Him. It doesn't matter if you've gone to church every week since you were a baby, or only saw the inside of a sanctuary for weddings and funerals.

Maybe the worst sin you can remember was when you were five years old and told your parents, "I didn't hit my brother." You're pretty righteous and really don't see that you need forgiveness. That attitude can be dangerous. It amounts to pride in your own ability to please God, but no matter how good you are, it's not enough. The Bible addresses that in Isaiah:

> All of us have become like one who is unclean, and all our righteous acts are like filthy rags (Isaiah 64:6 NIV).

Paul says in Romans 3:23: "All have sinned and fall short of the glory of God." In other words, we're all sinners. None of us are good enough on our own.

Maybe your situation is just the opposite. You may have been totally messed up with drugs or cheated on your spouse or committed crimes that sent you to prison. Now you wonder if God can possibly forgive you. 1 John 1:9 assures us:

> If we confess our sins, He is faithful and just to forgive us our sins and to cleanse us from all unrighteousness.

Trust Him. It doesn't matter how far away you've been. Even if we have trouble forgiving ourselves, He loves each of us more than we can imagine. He is eager to forgive us. The Lord wants to welcome us into His family as soon as we stop doing things our own way and begin to follow Him. What matters is that we put our confidence in Jesus, not our own abilities. That prepares us for the awesome things He has in store.

So, if you're ready to give God your earthly life, He is ready to give you eternal life. You may want to find a quiet place where you can talk to Him in your own words. Be real. He already knows everything about you. Ask Jesus to forgive your sins, because they stand between you and Him. He may bring specific things to your mind that you need to talk to Him about. Nothing is beyond forgiveness when you humbly come to Christ Jesus. Tell Him you need Him and want Him to be your Lord. Invite Him to come into your life and take over. Let God do what only He can do. Then thank Him.

When I lead people into a relationship with Jesus, I ask them to repeat a prayer that goes something like this:

> *God, I've been going my own way, doing my own thing. I've filled my life with other things and ignored You. I've sinned against You, but I'm through playing games. I need You in my life. You know my past, my pain, my shame—I believe you took the penalty for my rebellion. I don't want to hide anything from You. I open myself up to You and ask You to clean up the messes I've made. I need Your forgiveness. I put my faith in You, Lord. Please take my life and make me whole. Come live in me and do a new work in my heart. You're God and I'm not, so I choose to obey You from now on. Thank You for everything You've promised, Lord!*

If you sincerely mean that, from your heart, you can be absolutely sure that Jesus Christ has forgiven you and come to dwell in you. You may feel something special or you may not. Feelings come and go, but you can always depend on the truth of God's Word.

Now What?

As soon as you are part of the family of God, you're ready to go further and receive the baptism in the Holy Spirit. I encourage you to dive in—receive the gift He longs to give. Remember he is a loving Father who wants to give good gifts to His kids.

We've already talked about who this gift is for, but it's worth repeating. The baptism in the Holy Spirit is available to every Christian, everywhere, throughout every age. The first people to follow Jesus were Jews, and some of them were shocked when the Lord accepted others into His family and filled them with the Holy Spirit. So if you're Jewish, accepting Jesus as your Messiah and being filled with the Holy Spirit doesn't mean you stop being a Jew. Instead, it adds depth and resolve to your life. You'll be more complete.

Denominational differences don't matter to God, either. You may have been raised as a Baptist or Lutheran, Catholic or Presbyterian, or nothing at all. Like me, you may not have grown up with any church experiences. Whatever your past, the Lord is waiting to bless your future.

Just to be sure you know you're not disqualified because of anything in your spiritual background, look at Galatians 3:14.

> Through Christ Jesus, God has blessed the Gentiles with the same blessing he promised

to Abraham, so that we who are believers might receive the promised Holy Spirit through faith. (NLT)

In the Bible, the word "Gentiles" referred to everyone who wasn't Jewish. Some were even involved in all sorts of pagan practices, but that didn't block God's love or cause Him to decide those people didn't deserve His gifts.

Now, if you want the gift of the Holy Spirit, prayerfully think about these things:

- Jesus promised the Holy Spirit to His followers—that includes you, if you have received Him as your Savior. He's eager to give everything you need to be victorious.
- Open your heart, your innermost being, in an act of surrender to Him. Relinquish every bit of yourself to the Lord.
- Specifically ask Jesus to baptize you—to immerse and saturate you with the Holy Spirit.
- Expect Him to start a transformation process in you, from the inside out.
- Begin to thank God for giving you what He promised. Talk to Him, sing praises, shout, clap, get on your knees or on your face, walk around, dance, or sit quietly and listen— whatever helps you focus on God.
- If you sense words forming as you worship Him, let them come out. Don't try to work up a new language, but don't be surprised or

intimidated if your praise is deeper than any words you've ever learned.

You can talk to the Lord in your own words, or if you want a guideline, here's a prayer to follow to request baptism in the Holy Spirit:

> *Dear Lord Jesus, thank You for everything You've already done in my life. Now I come to You in obedience and ask You to baptize me with Your Holy Spirit. I know I need the Helper to fill me and give me power to be a good witness of Your magnificence. I want to overflow with the confident hope You promise, and to be so full of Your Spirit that everyone I'm with will feel Your love. I open myself totally to You, to receive everything You want to give. I praise You for who You are and for all You do. Help me glorify You with every part of my life. I love You! Praise You Jesus!*

You may feel overwhelmed with a fresh awakening in your spirit, and adoration will soar beyond anything you've known before. You could receive a prayer language as you praise the Lord, and speak your love for Him with words you never learned. I'll talk about that more in Chapter 16. Or you may not feel any different, and wonder if anything has really happened. Regardless of how you *feel*, remember that Jesus promised to give the Holy Spirit to those who ask. We ask for this gift and receive it by faith, just like salvation. Trust Him, whether you feel different or not.

Receiving the baptism in the Holy Spirit doesn't mean you have arrived. It's the beginning of an exciting new leg of your journey with Christ. Every day, for the rest of your life, you can go further, and your relationship with Him will grow deeper and more intimate.

Jude 1:20-21 says:

> But you, beloved, building yourselves up on your most holy faith, praying in the Holy Spirit, keep yourselves in the love of God, looking for the mercy of our Lord Jesus Christ unto eternal life.

Every day, God will build your faith. Praying in the Holy Spirit is a natural building block that helps us stay in the midst of God's love and mercy as He prepares us for eternity.

Do you want to overflow with supernatural power? The baptism in the Holy Spirit is essential to fulfill that desire. As you study the Bible and pray, you'll discover the truth of God's promises. You can always trust Him!

The Holy Spirit releases the miracle-life of Jesus to work through us. You may be set free from some sin or addiction that has bound you for a long time that you were powerless to change on your own. You could experience healing, or freedom from anger or fear. You might receive a word of wisdom or knowledge to help someone else. Be open—God will continually amaze you. Be willing to overflow with joy and peace and hope.

Say, "Overflow!"

14

Overflow Happens

You may wonder, *How will I know I'm filled with the Holy Spirit? What should I expect?* I can guarantee that as you grow in this new reality, you will experience God working in your life. You may be more aware of His presence and want to please Him like never before. When you read the Bible, Scriptures will "come alive" and you will understand how things in God's Word relate to your own life. Your prayer life may change as you learn to talk with Him about everything, like you would talk to a loving father or your best friend.

So, you're diligently trying to follow Him. You

want to have the kind of faith that pleases God. You want to overflow with confident hope, and be a powerful witness. How does that work in real life, outside the church walls? You know what I mean. Maybe you enjoy a fantastic worship time with other believers each weekend and get pumped-up from the pastor's powerful message. Then Monday comes. Your family thinks you're totally out of touch, your job doesn't feel very secure, and news from Washington D.C. or Wall Street leaves you depressed. It's rough.

Think again about Paul's message of overflow:

> I pray that God, the source of hope, will fill you completely with joy and peace because you trust in him. Then you will overflow with confident hope through the power of the Holy Spirit (Romans 15:13 NLT).

That Scripture is near the end of Paul's letter to Roman believers, and I think the church in America has a lot in common with them. Rome was a dominant power, like the United States is today. Roman citizens came from varied ethnic and religious backgrounds. Some were wealthy and well-educated, while others struggled to provide the basic necessities for their families. Their differences and diversities sometimes caused conflict, even among believers. Does that sound familiar?

As the Spirit of God began to influence Rome and the gospel impacted people, the church grew. God did fantastic things. It's exciting to see how He brought people together from every walk of life and united them with a single purpose, but that caused opposition from the government. No wonder the Roman leaders saw these zealous Christians as a threat. They were willing to give up everything, even their lives, rather than renounce their faith in Jesus as the Messiah, their Savior. That troubled the rulers.

Christians face similar resistance now, even in our nation, as it becomes less and less politically correct to believe that the Bible is the Word of God. Because of the similarities, Paul's prayer for believers in Rome seems very appropriate for you and me.

Remember the definition of *overflow*. It means to spill out over the limits or edge of a container because the container is too full. My thesaurus lists synonyms like: run over, flood, spread out, and spill over. As a noun, overflow suggests excess with more to spare, extra, or surplus. The opposite of overflow is lack or deficiency.

Paul prayed that Christians would overflow with confident hope through the power of the Holy Spirit because they trust in Him. God doesn't want His people to live on the brink of defeat. His heart's desire—His passion—is that we all *overflow* with hope.

How to Overflow

The Holy Spirit wants to go with us, and overflow from us, wherever we are. Imagine being so completely full of the Holy Spirit that joy, peace, and confident hope slosh out of our lives and splash onto people around us. That will happen if we're tuned in to Him every day, whatever we do, wherever we go. He is always as near as our next thought.

What would it look like to overflow with God's Spirit when we're at work, with our families, and in our neighborhoods? Suppose every time we're at a grocery store, a parent-teacher conference, or in line at the DMV to renew a driver's license, we're so full we can't contain Him. Then people won't just see us, they'll see the Lord in us. They'll sense the heart of Jesus and experience the love of God just because we're there. That's what the Holy Spirit longs for.

In Acts 4 we read about a time when Peter and John were in trouble with the Jewish authorities. By the power of the Holy Spirit working through them, they healed a lame man and a crowd gathered to hear them preach about Jesus. The priests, Sadducees, and the captain of the temple guard were "greatly disturbed," and arrested them. The next day the rulers demanded that they explain by what power they preached and healed. Peter saw that as an opportunity; he didn't hesitate to speak up:

> "If we this day are judged for a good deed done to a helpless man, by what means he has been made well, let it be known to you all, and to all the people of Israel, that by the name of Jesus Christ of Nazareth, whom you crucified, whom God raised from the dead, by Him this man stands here before you whole … Nor is there salvation in any other, for there is no other name under heaven given among men by which we must be saved" (Acts 4:9-10, 12).

That didn't earn Peter any points with the leaders, but they saw undeniable boldness in these men. Acts 4:13 says:

> Now when they saw the boldness of Peter and John, and perceived that they were un-

educated and untrained men, they marveled. And they realized that they had been with Jesus.

Even in that threatening situation, Peter and John overflowed with God's presence so much their enemies knew they had been with Jesus. Do you want people to see Jesus in you? I do!

This overflow isn't something we can work up on our own. Bookstore shelves are loaded with self-help books that tell us how to be more organized, more patient, more confident, more intentional, and all sorts of other good traits. They promote behavioral changes that may be good, at least temporarily, but that's not what God is looking for.

He wants our hearts to be totally transformed, and that only happens when we spend time with Him and trust Him to do what He promises. Only the Creator can recreate us into overflowing vessels.

The fruit of the Spirit is listed in Galatians 5:22-23: love, joy, peace, patience, kindness, goodness, faithfulness, gentleness, and self-control. Those attributes don't come from winning the rat race, from financial security, or from having lots of college degrees tagged onto our names. A loving family, a beautiful home, or a perfect job can't produce a supernatural overflow of the Spirit.

The list of spiritual fruit can be intimidating when we compare it to what we see in our own lives. Or when we think about what other people see in us. The only way to overflow with authentic love, peace, and joy is through a dynamic, intimate relationship with Jesus. When we stay connected to Him through the power of the Holy Spirit, our lives will be full and we will glorify God wherever we are.

We're born again when we surrender to Jesus. His gift works with our faith. We receive the baptism in the Holy Spirit the same way: He gives and we receive. That principle doesn't change as we continue to grow spiritually.

Strong, Spirit-filled Christians don't strut across the stage of life, proud of their own accomplishments. Spiritual giants are humble, totally dependent on the Lord to give everything they need and even a surplus. The more we overflow with the presence of the Holy Spirit, the more we realize how inadequate we are on our own. The only way we can be everything He wants us to be is to be involved with Him constantly.

Learn to Follow

When the Holy Spirit leads, it's our job to follow, but that doesn't necessarily come easily. That became clear to me one day when I was stuck behind a really, really slow car. The elderly couple ahead of me seemed to debate at every intersection whether or not to turn. Then they'd creep forward. I couldn't pass them, and I was getting impatient.

After a few blocks we stopped at a light and the lady opened her door and got out and headed back to my car with a little scrap of paper. I rolled down my window, and she showed me the note, with directions to a softball field. She said, "Our granddaughter has a ball game, but we can't find this place. Can you help us?"

They were way off course. I started to tell her how to get there but I really didn't think they'd find it.

So I said, "Follow me. I'll show you the way."

She walked back, climbed in her car, and they let me take the lead, but they didn't keep up. I kept checking my rearview mirror to be sure they were still there. They followed so far behind it seemed like the man might have said, "I'll follow him, but I'm really not sure he's taking us where we want to go."

I'd get ahead and wait for them to catch up, then we'd drive a little farther, and I'd slow down till they caught up again. I was thinking, *Come on! The game's started by now. You'll miss the whole thing if you don't get moving.* I eventually got them there, but it was a frustrating experience.

Could we be that way with the Holy Spirit sometimes? We follow, but we're not absolutely sure He's taking us where we want to go. We're coming, but maybe we wonder, *Are You sure this is the right way?*

Do you suppose the Holy Spirit might think, *Come on! The game's started—you'll miss the whole thing if you don't get moving.*

Learning to follow Him is a process, but this is the beginning of an exciting adventure.

God's promises are true. He loves us and has good plans for us. He wants us to reach out and take everything He offers. We ask. God gives. We receive. God does the supernatural (lead), and we do the natural (follow). Then our lives can overflow with God's very best.

Say, "Overflow!"

15

Gifts of the Spirit

In the Apostle Paul's first letter to the Corinthians, he lists the gifts of the Spirit and explains their purpose:

> But the manifestation of the Spirit is given to each one for the profit of all: for to one is given the word of wisdom through the Spirit, to another the word of knowledge through the same Spirit, to another faith by the same Spirit, to another gifts of healings by the same Spirit, to another

the working of miracles, to another
prophecy, to another discerning of
spirits, to another different kinds of
tongues, to another the interpretation
of tongues. But one and the same
Spirit works all these things,
distributing to each one individually as
He wills (1 Corinthians 12:7-11).

Did you notice the first sentence of this Scripture
says the gifts are given for the profit of all? That
means we are to use the gifts to benefit others and to
help build up the kingdom of God. We don't open
ourselves to the Holy Spirit to flaunt our standing as
one of God's special agents. The more we love Him,
the more we care about the people around us, and
that makes us want to see others grow closer to Him.
The gifts of the Spirit infuse us with spiritual power
so we can minister to our family, friends, and anyone
else the Lord sends our way. It's part of the overflow.

If you believe God wants to see the gifts of the
Spirit revealed in you, and you know they are
available, the real question is whether or not *you* are
available. The Holy Spirit isn't reserved for the super-
spiritual. You don't have to be an evangelist or a
pastor for the power of the Holy Spirit to overflow
from your life onto others. You just have to be
willing. "Here I am coach! Send me into the game."

The Bible says Jesus is the same today as He was
2,000 years ago, and He will never change (Hebrews
13:8). He yearns for each believer to receive the gifts
of the Spirit now, just like the New Testament
Christians. The Holy Spirit will equip everyone who
wants Christ's heart to be manifested through us to

others. If we love God and desire to touch people with His compassion, we're candidates for the supernatural. He will give us spiritual gifts if we open ourselves completely to Him.

When we overflow, people will sense the love of God in us. The Apostle Paul tells us to allow the gifts of the Spirit to work through us, always backed with love.

> Though I speak with the tongues of men and of angels, but have not love, I have become sounding brass or a clanging cymbal. And though I have the gift of prophecy, and understand all mysteries and all knowledge, and though I have all faith, so that I could remove mountains, but have not love, I am nothing. And though I bestow all my goods to feed the poor, and though I give my body to be burned, but have not love, it profits me nothing (1 Corinthians 13:1-3).

This Scripture begins with the gifts of the Spirit, and reminds us that everything we do should be motivated by love. Nothing in those verses implies the gifts of the Spirit aren't important. What the Lord wants to impress on our hearts is that love is essential in order for the gifts to accomplish His purpose.

The next chapter follows the same theme. In 1 Corinthians 14:1, Paul says,

> "Let love be your highest goal! But you should also pursue the special abilities the Spirit gives" (NLT).

Let's look into a couple of the gifts.

The Gift of Prophecy

Prophets of the Old Testament tried to prepare Israel for things to come. They continually warned people of the consequences if they continued to worship idols and turn away from the God of their fathers. Sometimes the prophets were able to convince people to repent; other times it seemed like no one paid any attention.

God can still speak through people in that way. But most of the time when the gift of prophecy is used in the New Testament it refers to "edification, exhortation, and comfort," as Paul said in 1 Corinthians 14:3.

The gift of prophecy is meant to benefit others with anointed words of encouragement, insight, direction, and affirmation. It can be given by a pastor, but God isn't limited. He can work through anyone to stir up expectation and keep people from being apathetic.

Paul said, "Pursue love, and desire spiritual gifts, but especially that you may prophesy." Some people think that statement in 1 Corinthians 14:1 implies that the other gifts are less important, but I don't believe that was what Paul intended. All spiritual gifts are valuable and need to be built on a foundation of love. But in a worship service, the Holy Spirit can use prophecy to exhort and encourage an entire congregation. That means the gift of prophecy would be more beneficial in that setting than some of the other gifts.

Supernatural Wisdom and Knowledge

When we need wisdom or knowledge beyond our own abilities for a specific situation, the Holy Spirit provides it. I've experienced this in my own life and I've received from others who heard an explicit word from God for me.

In 2002, my wife Mary and I were serving at a church in Michigan. Before that, I was a youth pastor in Shawnee, Kansas for several years and we had been on the mission field. We loved what God was doing throughout that time, but we began to sense Him leading us into something new.

I was comfortable working with youth and never really wanted to be a senior pastor. I have to admit, I came up with excuses when the Lord showed us He wanted us to return to Kansas to start LifeMission Church. I didn't feel qualified. But in a deeper way, we knew it was right.

The pastors I worked with in Michigan agreed that it was God's plan, and prayed for us as we prepared to move. The senior pastor, Duane Vander Klok, stepped in front of me as he prayed and said, "Clint, I think God has a word for you." He went on, "You've been faithful in other men's fields. Now God is giving you a field you didn't plant, and it's going to be a fruitful field for generations to come." Then he moved on to pray for others. I knew this man had been living with the Holy Spirit's overflow for years, so speaking as the Lord prompted wasn't anything new to him.

I didn't understand exactly what it meant, but by faith Mary and I planned and strategized and headed home to Kansas.

Our dream was to share the gospel with young

families in a setting where they could be nurtured and become strong in their faith. After we were settled, a few friends got together with us at our house to pray about God's direction for LifeMission Church. Several basic values became clear. We wanted to provide authentic worship, genuine community, local outreach, world missions and creative communication. Of course, ministry to youth and children was vital. Those were the priorities God gave us.

We found a school to rent for Sundays and started meeting there. From the very first service people got saved and the church grew. Before long we moved to a bigger school. Within about six months, almost 100 people had given their lives to Christ and the average attendance was close to 200.

Then one day some leaders of a local church we had been renting space from wanted to meet with me. They had "planted" their "field." Through the years they gave sacrificially and prayed and built the church. But they had been without a pastor for over a year and were beginning to struggle. When we talked and prayed together, we all sensed that God wanted us to combine our two congregations.

It's been amazing! We moved into their building, and the very first Sunday more than 300 people came to LifeMission Church. From the beginning, our church had a heart for missions; ten percent of every offering goes to support missionaries and the work they do around the world. God continues to add people, and with a growing congregation our vision for ministry and outreach also keeps growing. We love to welcome people who are searching for a deep, meaningful relationship with the Lord.

Now over 2,500 attend LifeMission Church each

week, and last year more than 400 came forward to receive Jesus Christ as Lord and Savior. We've seen marriages healed, families restored, addictions broken, and people experience other amazing miracles. In 2008 we built a larger building to make room for the people God sends. We added an extension campus and planted a church in another town. I say this to illustrate that we are seeing a "great harvest," in a "field" I didn't plant, just like Pastor Duane said. Don't tell me the supernatural isn't active today!

It's humbling and incredibly exciting to be part of a work the Lord is doing. God spoke through the power of the Holy Spirit to one of His servants and we are seeing those words actually happen.

How the Gifts Work Together

All the gifts are necessary and to be used to build up the whole church. Sometimes the gifts can overlap or intertwine. The message Pastor VanderKlok spoke when he prayed for me was a word of knowledge, but it was also prophetic.

Peter wrote to Christians living in various areas in Asia Minor:

> As each one has received a gift, minister it to one another, as good stewards of the manifold grace of God (1 Peter 4:10).

Paul had a similar admonition for those in Rome. I like the *New Living Translation* of Romans 12:6-10:

> In his grace, God has given us different gifts for doing certain things well. So if God has given you the ability to prophesy, speak out

with as much faith as God has given you. If your gift is serving others, serve them well. If you are a teacher, teach well. If your gift is to encourage others, be encouraging. If it is giving, give generously. If God has given you leadership ability, take the responsibility seriously. And if you have a gift for showing kindness to others, do it gladly. Don't just pretend to love others. Really love them. Hate what is wrong. Hold tightly to what is good. Love each other with genuine affection, and take delight in honoring each other.

A healthy church allows the Holy Spirit to work through the gifts to minister to the people, being careful that all things are done in order and that Jesus is always glorified. God's purpose for each believer is for us to reach out to meet the needs of one another as we overflow with the power of the Holy Spirit.

Say, "Overflow!"

16

What About Tongues?

I pray that you will be open to experience the gifts of the Holy Spirit, including the gift of tongues. Praying in tongues is a resource to help us pray, praise, worship, and wage warfare. None of His gifts are given as a test to prove something has happened. We have the assurance in Scripture that when we ask, God gives.

Speaking in tongues is a spiritual gift that might scare some people. To anyone who hasn't been in a church that teaches the availability of the various gifts of the Spirit, the idea of praying in a language you don't know may seem strange. But for those who have received the gift, it is liberating, life-changing, and exciting. The Bible talks about this gift in several places throughout the New Testament, but there is still some misunderstanding regarding what it means to us today.

Some people receive a prayer language, or tongues, the moment they pray for the baptism in the Holy Spirit. Others may find themselves praying in tongues some time later, when they're caught up in praise and enjoying the presence of the Lord. It doesn't matter to God where you are. You could be kneeling in a beautiful sanctuary with sunlight streaming through stained glass windows or sitting in a battered old car. You might be watching waves roll in on a beach or vacuuming your living room. The Lord gives each of us a unique experience, tailor-made to perfectly fit our situation and personality.

The book of Acts tells the amazing story of outpouring of the Holy Spirit on the Day of Pentecost. In Acts 2:11 we read that the people in Jerusalem heard the new Spirit-filled believers speak in languages they had never learned. They glorified God and effectively communicated the gospel so that others heard the message in their own dialect. This was a miraculous occurrence that impacted everyone who experienced it. It is one of the events in history that makes me wish someone would get the whole time-machine thing figured out—I would really like to be there!

Incredible stories occasionally come from missionaries who experience the same kind of miracles today. They may be in a foreign culture where they haven't mastered the language, and God supernaturally gives them words to speak so the people understand. Is that awesome or what? It's like living the book of Acts in our generation.

Speaking in Tongues: In Public or Private Worship

It's important to understand that the Bible reveals two distinct purposes for the gift of tongues in the life of a believer. The first is the public use of tongues, when it is meant to either be interpreted by someone who has the gift of interpretation or heard by a group of people who speak that language. The latter was what people experienced on the Day of Pentecost.

The other purpose is more personal and is referred to as "praying in tongues" or "praying in the Spirit." Jude 1:20-21 tells us:

> But you, beloved, building yourselves up on your most holy faith, praying in the Holy Spirit, keep yourselves in the love of God, looking for the mercy of our Lord Jesus Christ unto eternal life.

This is a powerful gift in the life of believer and is meant to be a part of our daily spiritual growth experience.

Scripture makes it clear that both applications are available and distinct. The context and purpose of the gift of tongues shows whether the writer is talking about a public church service or private prayer.

It's interesting that in his first letter to the Corinthians, the Apostle Paul discourages the excessive use of tongues in public, while he encourages everyone to exercise the gift of tongues

privately. Praying in tongues in private prayer time
strengthens believers.

In 1 Corinthians 14:4-5, Paul said:

> A person who speaks in tongues is
> strengthened personally, but one who speaks
> a word of prophecy strengthens the entire
> church. I wish you could all speak in tongues,
> but even more I wish you could all prophesy.
> For prophecy is greater than speaking in
> tongues, unless someone interprets what you
> are saying so that the whole church will be
> strengthened (NLT).

Most of the time when we pray in tongues, God
gives us a "heavenly" language that no one
understands. We're praying to God, and He not only
knows what we say, the words come directly from His
Spirit. At times we may "hear" ourselves and think it
sounds like some language we've heard but never
learned. Whether we pray in an earthly language or an
angelic tongue, we can be sure we're praying a perfect
prayer that hasn't been filtered through our own
tainted thought processes.

Sometimes when I pray in tongues, the Holy
Spirit lets me know how to effectively help someone.
He may give me a word of knowledge or wisdom that
is exactly what that person needs at that particular
moment. Or God opens my mind to understand how
He wants me to pray, so I move from tongues to
English with confidence that He is directing the
prayer.

According to what we read in 1 Corinthians 14:5,
when a person has a message in tongues during a

church service, someone will receive an interpretation to build up the whole congregation. The person who speaks in tongues may also receive the interpretation, or it might come through another believer. 1 Corinthians 12:7-11 lists the various gifts of the Spirit that are used in the church:

> But the manifestation of the Spirit is given to each one for the profit of all; for to one is given the word of wisdom through the Spirit, to another the word of knowledge through the same Spirit, to another faith by the same Spirit, to another gifts of healings by the same Spirit, to another the working of miracles, to another prophecy, to another discerning of spirits, to another *different* kinds of tongues, to another the interpretation of tongues. But one and the same Spirit works all these things, distributing to each one individually as He wills.

Why Speak in Tongues?

As I stated earlier, the Apostle Paul sometimes referred to tongues as "praying in the Spirit." In Ephesians 6, he taught about spiritual warfare and the armor of God. He added, in verse 18:

> … praying always with all prayer and supplication in the Spirit, being watchful to this end with all perseverance and supplication for all the saints.

1 Corinthians 14:15 says:

> What is the conclusion then? I will pray with the spirit, and I will also pray with the understanding. I will sing with the spirit, and I will also sing with the understanding.

To Paul, praying and singing in tongues, or in the Spirit, was a normal experience for the people of the early church. And it can be for you, too. I know it is for me.

I pray in tongues every day when I worship, seek more of God, have big decisions to make, or when I intercede for others. Every time I prepare for ministry I need supernatural insight, and praying in the Spirit opens my spirit to God's wisdom.

I don't believe anyone *has* to speak in tongues, but we *get* to. It's an awesome privilege! God's Holy Spirit wants to direct our words beyond our own intellect. Speaking in tongues is not the only sign of being filled with the Holy Spirit. But it is from God, and why wouldn't Christians want everything He offers?

Alone with the Lord

In our own personal time with God, praying in tongues builds us up. The Apostle Paul said, "He who speaks in a tongue edifies himself …" And, "I thank my God I speak with tongues more than you all" (1 Corinthians 14:4, 18).

Paul must have prayed in tongues often when no one was with him and he was able to worship and talk to God alone. Paul wasn't bragging when he said he spoke in tongues more than the Corinthian Christians. He wanted to make it clear that he depended on the power of the Holy Spirit to help him live victoriously and accomplish the work God gave him. Paul faced incredible opposition from Jewish leaders, the government, and often even from other believers. He had to be continually strengthened.

We don't have the same concerns Paul did, but everyone needs to be built up spiritually all the time. Does that sound selfish? Not at all! In order to minister to others, we must be strong. No one who's barely able to hang on can be much help to anyone else. By praying in tongues throughout the day, our spirits will stay strong and ready for whatever the Lord arranges.

Intercessory Prayer

When we pray in the Spirit we are praying the will of God by the power of the Holy Spirit. Look at what Romans 8:26 says:

> Likewise the Spirit also helps in our weaknesses. For we do not know what we should pray for as we ought, but the Spirit Himself makes intercession for us with groanings which cannot be uttered.

Sometimes we just don't know how to pray for others. We can't possibly understand everything that's going on in another person's life. I'm not always sure about what is happening in my own situation, but I don't have to be. The Holy Spirit knows more about each of us than we know, even about ourselves. But when we pray in tongues we have the assurance that we're praying exactly what's needed. That's exciting!

Don't get hung up on speaking in tongues if it freaks you out. Instead, I want you to concentrate on your relationship with the Lord. Do you believe that everything He offers is because He loves us and wants to provide for our needs? If you're reluctant, give Him a chance to change your mind. Trust Him.

While I have only spent a little time on this subject, there are some very good books I recommend to anyone who would like to do more study. My top two picks would be: *The Beauty of Spiritual Language* by Jack Hayford, and *The God I Never Knew* by Robert Morris.

God longs for each of us to earnestly desire His gifts. It's all part of the overflow.

Say, "Overflow!"

17

Spirit-Empowered Day by Day

Jesus' ministry here on earth was clearly an overflow of the Holy Spirit, and it's obvious He wanted His followers to continue in the overflow. Through His Spirit, you and I can live with that same kind of victory each day. It's the life Jesus intended.

Think again about Jesus' baptism. Luke 4:1 says Jesus was filled with the Holy Spirit. They were already inseparably linked from before Jesus' birth, but at that moment, He was filled. Do you think that shows we need to be continually filled and refilled?

The same verse says He was led by the Spirit into the wilderness. His forty-day expedition into Satan's territory wasn't an accident. Jesus didn't just wander off and wind up in a lonely place with no food or water. He was led. Has it ever occurred to you when you're in a difficult situation, the Holy Spirit may have led you there? How you deal with the temptation determines whether you're teamed up with God's Spirit.

After the devil threw out every enticing lie he could come up with, trying to make Jesus stumble, the Lord returned from His ordeal in the power of the Holy Spirit (Luke 4:14). Jesus could have swallowed some of Satan's bait. But because He was filled, led, and empowered by the Holy Spirit, He was victorious when He emerged from the desert. Being tempted isn't sin. We can triumph over temptations as long as we aren't trying to handle them on our own.

If we don't invite the Holy Spirit to lead us, what does? It might be desires of our flesh, the lies of the enemy, fear of failure, concern about others' opinions, or fear of our own lack. What if Jesus had allowed any of those human reactions to take over? We can't comprehend the consequences. Our own decisions may not affect the course of history, but they can influence our families, careers, health, and any number of other things.

If you've opened your heart to receive Jesus and everything He offers, you're beginning to experience the joy of living close to Him. The more time you spend with Him in prayer and reading the Bible, the more you'll realize how much you need Him. Listen for His whisper. He will draw you into a deeper and deeper relationship with Him until you desperately long to please Him.

Nothing compares to the thrill of knowing we're being filled, led, and empowered by the same Spirit who filled, led, and empowered Jesus. Then we can be certain we're exactly where God wants us, fulfilling our purpose, and overflowing with His Spirit. He likes to put us in contact with people who need what we have to give. He equips us with spiritual gifts that are beyond our natural abilities, but precisely right for a particular moment.

Not a Do-It-Yourself Project

I've seen new believers set out with a burning conviction to give up their old habits and start fresh, but within a few weeks they're doing the same things they did before. Then they get discouraged and may wonder whether their experience was real. When we're full of the Holy Spirit, we don't have to be slaves to sin any longer. Maybe you've struggled with a particular sin for years. Most of us fight against things we can't conquer on our own. Check out Titus 2:11-12:

> For the grace of God has appeared that offers salvation to all people. It teaches us to say "No" to ungodliness and worldly passions, and to live self-controlled, upright and godly lives in this present age (NIV).

That's great news! We can win the battle over ungodliness when we learn to rely on God's grace and the power of the Holy Spirit. Sin keeps us from being healthy, overflowing believers. We can depend on the

Lord to rip that sin out of our lives by the roots.

If we try to remake ourselves, we come up against our own weakness. Only the power of the Holy Spirit can bring the changes He wants, when He wants. It's all about God, not our own abilities. He will transform us from the inside out.

The overflow starts when we accept Jesus as our Savior and pray to be filled with the Holy Spirit. But remember, that's only the beginning. Think about a container filled with liquid; if it just sits, it will become stagnant and eventually evaporate. It's the same for us. We can't expect to overflow if we aren't continually refilled. We need day-by-day refreshing if we're going to overflow with the joy, peace, and hope Jesus wants to give.

We've looked at how important this is to God. We can't be ho-hum about anything that is valuable to the Lord. He's a loving heavenly Daddy, always ready to fill us with good things so we will overflow and leave remnants of God wherever we go.

God is in Charge

Society conditions us to think we can determine our own destiny. We spend a lifetime building an image for ourselves and don't want anything to mess that up. We don't want to make ourselves vulnerable and we tend to be afraid of the unknown. Those attitudes can keep us from enjoying the incredible benefits of a life totally given over to Him. Throughout Scripture the Lord shows us He is trustworthy and longs to pour out blessings on anyone who will follow Him.

1 Corinthians 1:9 assures us:

> God will do this, for he is faithful to do what he says, and he has invited you into partnership with his Son, Jesus Christ our Lord (NLT).

Is that cool? God wants us to be partners with Jesus! Let that sink in. We can work together with the Creator of the universe to fill our part of the world with more of Him.

In 2 Thessalonians 3:3 we read:

> But the Lord is faithful, who will establish you and guard you from the evil one.

He wants to establish us. That makes me think of Him building something strong that can withstand the storms of life. There is nothing to fear when we put our trust in God. He is faithful and will protect us from Satan's schemes.

Every day can be an exciting adventure. If we let the Holy Spirit lead, He will prove that His plans for us are perfect and His love is unconditional. We can be absolutely sure that the Lord only wants what's best. I love Jeremiah 29:11:

> "For I know the plans I have for you," declares the Lord, "plans to prosper you and not to harm you, plans to give you hope and a future" (NIV).

His plans are so much better than anything we can come up with on our own. His imagination is boundless. He knows exactly what we need each moment, and how that will work together with other lives and circumstances to bring us to our ultimate goal. We only see a tiny fragment of eternity. We can't make it without Him.

A Holy Point of View

When Jesus fills us with His Spirit, our perspective begins to change. We start to see some things from God's point of view.

The Lord's desire is to fill us, lead us, and to empower us wherever we go. He wants to prepare us, so we're always ready and don't come up short. It doesn't make any difference what we did before. What's important is that we turn to Him in joyful obedience and let His Spirit guide us from now on.

God, our amazing coach, doesn't want us to settle for mediocrity. He wants us to have victory in every area of life—to win every game! The Lord encourages each of us to be active participants in life, and as He uses us to help other people we find complete satisfaction in His presence. Overflowing with peace and joy through the power of the Holy Spirit should become a fulfilling, vital part of life.

Do you see how much you need the Holy Spirit? Can you understand that when you receive this gift you enter a new dimension in your relationship with the Lord? He is eager to equip you as never before to do His work. He will prepare you to fulfill His purposes for you.

In the Gospel of John we read:

> On the last day, that great day of the feast, Jesus stood and cried out, saying, "If anyone

thirsts, let him come to Me and drink. He who believes in Me, as the Scripture has said, out of his heart will flow rivers of living water." This He spoke concerning the Spirit, whom those believing in Him would receive; for the Holy Spirit was not yet *given*, because Jesus was not yet glorified (John 7:37-39).

Jesus didn't just quietly say those words to a few people seated nearby. He "stood and cried out." He shouted, to make sure all the people heard and understood how important this was—that it was what He longed for. It was vitally important to them, and it's just as vital for us.

There is no limit on how much God will give. Every day we can trust Him to fill us until we overflow with more and more of Him. Rivers of living water can flow from our hearts to give life to others.

God wants everyone who loves Him to overflow with hope, joy and peace. When we're saturated with Him, our lives seem to burst with His Spirit. He wants to fill us, to lead us, and to empower us. As we allow Him to have His way, we'll leave a trace of God everywhere we go.

It's time to overflow!

I invite you to contact LifeMission Church if you have questions or need someone to pray with you.

LifeMission Church
16111 S Lone Elm Road
Olathe, KS 66062
(913) 829-7511
www.LifeMissionChurch.org

About the Authors

Clint Sprague is the Pastor of LifeMission Church in Olathe, Kansas. He spent thirteen years involved in missions and youth ministry before founding LifeMission Church in 2002. He is known for his authentic, practical, and inspiring communication style. Having been raised in a single parent home, Clint says his greatest joy in life is to honor God as a loving husband and a faithful father. His hobbies include dating his bride, playing with his kids, hanging out with friends, riding his motorcycle, anything sports related, and random acts of kindness. Follow Clint on Twitter: @CLINT_SPRAGUE

Ardythe Kolb is a freelance writer who has four books as well as hundreds of devotions, articles, and stories in various publications. She serves on the board of Heart of America Christian Writers' Network as editor of their monthly newsletter. She and her husband, Jerry, owned a Christian bookstore while raising their five children. Now, besides writing and spending time with family and friends, Ardythe volunteers as a Court Appointed Special Advocate for abused and neglected children. She also enjoys travel, reading, and target practice.

95707962R00075

Made in the USA
Columbia, SC
19 May 2018